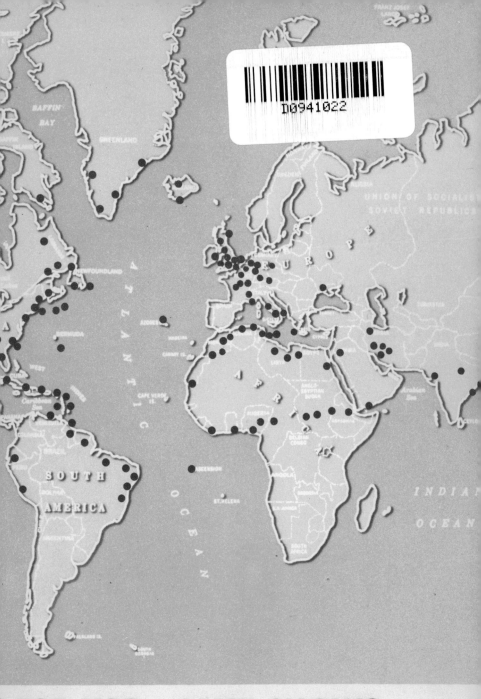

E FOR USO - CAMP SHOWS

vhich performances were given

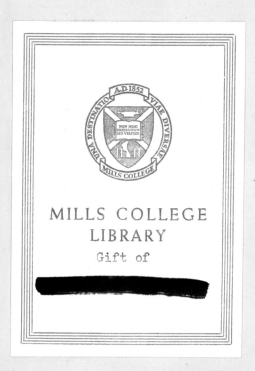

Home Away from Home

The Story of the USO

The

War and Navy
Department Department

express to the

United Service Organizations

their appreciation for patriotic service

The United Service Organizations, Inc., [USO] performed unique and outstanding services during World War II. In coordinating the religious, educational, and welfare services of its six national member agencies for the Armed Forces and for especially critical war production areas, it made a substantial contribution to the successful prosecution of the war and to the strengthening of the basic values of American democracy. It brought to a focus the resources of the amusement industry for the maintenance of the morale of American men and women on every fighting front. Its more than a million civilian men and women volunteers gave a nation-wide demonstration of uniquely effective cooperation.

Secretary of War   Secretary of the Navy

Washington, D.C., 1 May 1946

Home Away from Home

The Story of the USO

Julia M. (H. Carson)

Harper & Brothers *Publishers* New York & London

HOME AWAY FROM HOME

Copyright, 1946, by *Julia M. H. Carson*

PRINTED IN THE UNITED STATES OF AMERICA

FIRST EDITION

G-V

Contents

Illustrations

WAR DEPARTMENT
OFFICE OF THE CHIEF OF STAFF
WASHINGTON

Foreword to the Book Entitled

HOME AWAY FROM HOME - THE STORY OF USO

The war was won because of the cooperation of nations and of people within nations. The USO has given an impressive demonstration of the way people in our country of different creeds, races, and economic status can work together when the nation has dedicated itself to an all-out, integrated effort.

The people at home occupy a strategic place in a nation at war. One of their major responsibilities is to convince the armed forces that the country is behind them. In World War II this fact was brought home to military personnel by such service as the USO furnished in its clubs, station lounges, and through its mobile units. In addition, USO-Camp Shows brought American cheer and laughter close to every fighting front.

The USO served also in providing a channel through which more than a million civilian men and women were able to help effectively in the war effort. This cooperative, voluntary undertaking has been in line with our democratic way of life, and contributed greatly to victory.

DWIGHT D. EISENHOWER
General of the Army

NAVY DEPARTMENT
OFFICE OF THE CHIEF OF NAVAL OPERATIONS
WASHINGTON 25, D. C.

It gives me great pleasure to preface this book with a statement of the Navy's appreciation of the splendid service the USO has rendered to the personnel of the Navy, Marine Corps, and Coast Guard.

As Chief of the Bureau of Navigation in 1941, with responsibilities for the establishment of a comprehensive welfare and recreation program for Naval Personnel, I welcomed the formation of the United Service Organizations in February of that year. Later, as Commander-in-Chief of the Pacific Fleet and Pacific Ocean Areas I had the opportunity to observe the operations of many USO activities and to appreciate their outstanding contributions to the morale of the personnel of the Armed Forces under my command.

Throughout the war the USO performed an outstanding service both to the military and to the nation. Through the service of its professional staff and through its million volunteer workers it helped maintain a close bond of sympathy and understanding between the American people and their Armed Forces. This was an important contribution to the winning of the war.

The need for the USO in war time was emphatically demonstrated. While in peace time that need is reduced in scope, it will continue to be just as pressing for each individual bluejacket as it ever was. I know these men will face the same problems of healthful and constructive recreation that they faced during the war and I know that the USO can do much for the solution of these problems. I therefore congratulate the USO upon its decision to continue its work at strategic points until the end of 1947.

C.W. NIMITZ
Fleet Admiral, U. S. Navy.

Introduction

At the first mass meeting of the USO (the United Service Organizations, Incorporated) held in Washington on April 17, 1941, the essential features of the new organization were made clear by military and civilian leaders.

Six national Agencies were to compose it: the International Committee of Young Men's Christian Associations, the National Board of Young Women's Christian Associations, the National Catholic Community Service, The Salvation Army, the National Jewish Welfare Board, and The National Travelers Aid Association.

It was to be financed by the American people through voluntary contributions, not by Government funds.

Its work was to be under the general direction of the Army and the Navy. Its budgets were to be approved by the Government which in turn had agreed to erect some three hundred buildings for its use.

The USO's field of work is stated in its Constitution and By-Laws: "to aid in the war and defense program of the United States and its Allies by serving the religious, spiritual, welfare, and educational needs of the men and women in the armed forces and the war and defense industries of the United States and its Allies in the United States and throughout the world, and in general, to contribute to the maintenance of morale in American communities and elsewhere. . . ."

Clearly stated at the 1941 meeting also was a fundamental basis for the whole undertaking—a sharing of certain common faiths: belief "in a supernatural power that exists beyond any that is upon this earth; faith in the brotherhood of man; belief in the individual dignity of man; belief in the existence of positive ethical standards of right and wrong that exist apart from the will of any man. . . ."

At the peak of its work the USO had operations in every state. Over a five year period approximately $200,000,000 have been expended. Attendance figures exceed a billion. Over a million volunteers have given their services. To make possible the management of so extensive an undertaking, the six Agencies composing the USO have made available to it trained personnel, physical facilities, and the experience of years of social welfare work.

From its inception the USO has encountered difficulties implicit in its set-up and in the role it chose to play. Problems of sheer volume are involved in an enterprise growing from an original budget of $10,765,000 in 1941 to one approximately five times as large in 1945. Complex also have been matters of equipment and supply in a period of priorities and rationing. Central accounting, with such a number of local budgets involved, has been an undertaking of vast proportions.

Further, complications are inevitable when a private agency such as the USO deals with Governmental agencies and with the military. Nor have constructive attitudes always been easy to maintain in the delicate balance between lay and professional work. Ingenuity and patience have been required in working out satisfactory procedures involving the three faiths. Again different races, each represented in the country's fighting forces, have posed their own problems. For efficient functioning and for careful expenditure of funds contributed by the public, certain procedures have been required. Effort has been made to develop these procedures without stultifying the originality and freshness of approach necessary to keep the organization from becoming institutionalized.

In this book the religious aspects of work done in connection with the USO have not been given a separate chapter. There are two reasons for this: first, religious activities have been primarily the responsibility of the individual religious Agencies composing the USO and therefore any comprehensive account of their specialized variety and extent is a subject for treatment by the Protestant, Catholic, and Jewish member Agencies respectively; in the second place, the religious connotations of USO work germane to this story have been part of the total USO fabric, and it has therefore seemed appropriate to indicate some of them in descriptions of the undertaking as a whole.

Little of the evolution of the USO will appear on the surface of this book though it is implicit in its substructure. This book is, as the title indicates, the story of the USO, not a history, not an analytical account. It is written in terms of people, as the work itself was done. The people are fictitious characters who might have helped in the USO. The story told is true, however, chiseled as closely as possible to the spirit of the undertaking.

If, for those who have encountered what they believe to be the USO's short-comings, the story seems too much on the positive side, it can only be said that the description of any hard-bitten and determined effort with a surge of driving power behind it is bound to show the thing as a going concern. There have been in this organization no fewer blunders or failures of ideals than in any other finely conceived enterprise that the country as a whole has undertaken. The interesting fact is that the USO has surmounted them to produce a short-time demonstration (1941–1947) of what people of widely differing convictions, points of view and beliefs can accomplish together when they have made up their minds to get it done.

A book of this sort could not have been written without the generous assistance of many people who, knowingly or not, have contributed to it in conferences, in letters, and in reports. I gratefully acknowledge their help and also my indebtedness to bulletins, reports, memoranda, and other publications of the member Agencies of the USO. From these, as from various official documents of the USO itself, I have occasionally taken material directly, without specific indication of the source. I trust that this limited plagiarism, which has seemed to me unavoidable in this type of book, will be taken in good part.

For the method of presentation I take full responsibility.

National USO Headquarters   Julia M. H. Carson
350 Fifth Avenue   *Historian for the USO*
New York 1, New York
March 1946

Home Away from Home

The Story of the USO

CHAPTER I

On the Way

The thermometer on the way-station platform registered 103° as the
long transcontinental train slowed to a stop. Passengers, military and
civilian, inert for the last hundred miles of desert as though drugged
with the heat, bestirred themselves. They would get off and stretch
their legs—anything for a change.

"How long'll we be here, conductor?" Down the train steps they
came, hastily letting go of the hot iron handrail if, by mistake, they
had grasped it.

"Fifteen or twenty minutes." The conductor pushed his cap far
back and mopped his forehead with a limp white handkerchief as he
stood for a moment near several blocks of ice dripping on a hand truck
by the tracks. Under the fierce glare of the sun the air above the long
wooden platform quivered.

"Where can we get a drink?"

Meanwhile the USO canteen, half way down the platform, had
come to its toes from a brief moment of relaxation. The lull before
the train had thundered in had been only a temporary pause between
one period of rush and the next. Since four o'clock that morning
trucks, coming toward the station from a radius of a hundred miles,
had seen familiar signs, *USO cookies ready,* propped along the highway. Slowing down, they had picked up box after box and had

brought them to the canteen where Senior Hostesses were busy tying bundles of magazines, measuring out powdered coffee, getting everything in readiness for the moment of the train's arrival.

Twenty minutes ahead, the Commanding Officer on the approaching express telegraphed them he had two hundred and fifty ablebodied men aboard for cold drinks, and thirty hospitalized men for coffee and magazines. Since then, the orange and lemon squeezers had been running at a dizzy rate. The coffee was easier because the railroad had piped in hot steam, making boiling water almost instantaneous.

With everything ready several minutes before the train came into view, more than one housewife in a fresh cotton print with a USO armband above her left elbow, glanced at the walls of the little building where post cards from every battle front had been tacked—cards of thanks sent by boys who had had a snack here while the train was watered. The biggest rush order had been the day they had fed nine hundred people in one hour, and had made the sandwiches during the same sixty minutes!

It made one feel "in on things," they were thinking as they waited, having a chance to talk with boys who went on to Guam, Murmansk, le Havre, to flying the hump in China. And several women, looking nearer home, admitted their pleasant surprise at finding how many fine people there were in this local radius of a hundred miles, people they'd somehow never become acquainted with before.

Here was the train—at last!

"Helen, tell those girls to wheel the coffee cart far down the platform. The hospital cars'll be on the end, most likely. Caution them again not to do anything until the Commanding Officer tells them. Hey, wait a minute! You've forgotten the biggest package of comics!"

For a split-second the cold drinks stood in orderly rows and the cookies were piled high in stout, round baskets. But only for a second. Then out of the troop-sleepers poured a stream of khaki and a roar of cheerful noise. The cold drinks and the piles of cookies vanished as though a magician had waved his stick above them. Generous replacements continued to meet the same fate.

Far down the platform by the steps of a hospital car a medical attendant beckoned to a Junior Hostess in a blue and white checked dress. "Don't you want to walk up to the third window from the front of this car and grin at the sergeant inside? He's in an awful funk. We're going to pull him through in pretty good shape, but he won't believe it. Not much wonder, I suppose, with that great cast around him. What he needs is something new to think about. Try anything— even making faces might help."

Up ahead lying lengthwise of the third window the young Marine sergeant was not feeling so tough as he pretended. It was pretty decent of them, he knew, to turn him so he could watch the country change from farm land to mountains to desert. He had not traveled in this part of the country before and he had been curious. For some time, though, the monotony and the distances to which he was not accustomed had been making him tired. If only there were something to look at close by. But when they stopped at the way-station, he had shut his eyes. He could do without seeing the pity in other peoples'.

Presently a fingernail tapped on his window with a gay rhythm and he could not help looking. Outside a girl in a blue and white checked dress was gazing at him without the least pity in her friendly, round face.

"Hello, Marine!" she called. "Bet you can't do this!"

He could barely hear her through the thick glass and above the pervading din but it was nice to have her there. She looked like the kid sister he often wished he had.

Now she was holding up four odd-shaped scraps of paper. Suddenly they made the letter "T" on her flattened palm. She let him have one brief look, then shuffled the pieces together. "Bet you can't do it!"

"Bet I can!"

"O.K., smartie. Go ahead and try. I'll send the pieces in."

For several minutes she watched him arrange and rearrange the scraps of papers on the window sill. She saw no "T" emerging but a firm jaw set with determination. Good! It was a tricky little puzzle and should keep him occupied for some few minutes. Tapping on the window again, she thrust out the tip of her tongue in a cheerful I-told-you-so, and waved goodbye. He grinned, gave her a half salute, then concentrated on the puzzle in the immediate foreground. If he hadn't seen it done—

Meanwhile, in the midst of the mob at the canteen a spoon was suddenly rapped against a tray. A little gray-haired woman called into the abrupt silence, "Is it anybody's birthday?"

"It's mine, ma'am."

"It's mine!"

"It's my son's too," she told them and her eyes were shining. "He's a Seabee in the South Pacific. Will you all help eat his birthday cake?"

She struck a match and twenty-nine candles flared. "Now you two each make a wish and blow." Deftly she cut the cake—a devil's food with thick white icing—and felt her son's thanks in their noisy appreciation.

All aboard came the warning.

* * * * *

Boarding the train here was a Mrs. Rufus Brown, a national director of the USO. She had been visiting her married daughter some twenty miles from this way-station when a letter had come from national headquarters asking if she would undertake a rapid survey of the variety and scope of services being furnished by the USO to military personnel and their families on the move. For years she had been interested in problems connected with transients, and while she had no high opinion of her qualifications for such a survey, the assignment was much to her taste.

Telephoning the station on the chance that she might pick up a cancellation, she was told she could have an upper that same afternoon. Such prompt departure made her schedule a little stiff, but five minutes before the train pulled out she was aboard though she did not have time to pin her volunteer USO pin to her jacket until she was seated backward in the Pullman.

Looking up from fastening the pin she saw her seat-mate, a substantial girl in her early twenties, turn in from the aisle with a fat and cheerful baby on her arm.

"Oh, I'm so glad you're from the USO," cried the young mother. "We've been traveling three days. This'll be the third night. Susan is an angel but traveling with a child gets awfully monotonous. Her daddy's due back from overseas and we've come clear across the continent to see him. Would you be willing to hold Susan while I go stand in line for the diner? I haven't had a peaceful meal since we left home."

"Certainly," said Mrs. Rufus Brown.

Receiving the solid, healthy weight of Susan, Mrs. Brown told herself it was appropriate she should begin her trip by helping a soldier's wife. It was true that taking care of children, other than her own, had never been her favorite pastime. However, she added as cordially as she could, "Susan and I will make out perfectly. Don't give us a thought."

"Oh, Susan's never any trouble to anybody," she was reassured as distinctly as generous applications of lipstick would permit.

Two hours later, when the girl returned, she found her child sleeping peacefully. "My mother's a great hustler for the USO," she announced as though offering Mrs. Brown something in return for her vigilance. "We live near a railroad junction and often there's three or four hours in the middle of the night between passenger trains." She explained that at first servicemen were just stranded there with nothing to do except to sit the night out in the dim station on hard wooden benches. Then her mother and father and some other couples decided to take turns meeting the two a.m. express. When it departed, leaving a disgruntled bunch of boys behind, her father or one of the other men would sing out, "How about coming up to the USO, boys? The ladies have got the ice-box full of stuff for sandwiches, and I shouldn't wonder if there were a couple of gallons of cold milk. We'll see you get back here in plenty of time to catch the five-fourteen."

Mrs. Brown, gathering up her bag and a magazine preparatory to going to the diner herself, didn't have to be told that it meant a lot to those boys to be remembered in the middle of the night. She knew, too, that the men and women who met the trains were glad of a chance to help, no matter how tired or worried they might be. It helped ease the tension in these difficult days of strain when there were stars in so many peoples' windows. And there was the feeling also that as they helped in one place, somewhere else their own boys were being provided for.

As she walked through the aisle, swaying with the train, she thought how exactly right it was that the sort of service the USO was providing should be given by the people themselves as civilians and not by the Government. The boys' leisure time needed to be as free as possible from regimentation. They needed to feel that the people as fathers and mothers, as families and friends, were interested in them as individuals and anxious to give them a hand whenever they could.

Walking well toward the end of the long train, Mrs. Brown discovered she could get no closer to food than the platform outside the diner. Ahead of her in line was a corporal who looked more like a friendly, overgrown boy than a seasoned fighter in spite of his overseas ribbon. He offered several remarks about the weather and the unpleasant traveling conditions, and when, in the course of half an hour, they reached the diner entrance, he asked suddenly, "Would you mind if I sat with you, ma'am? My name's Corporal Hudson, Robert Hudson."

She assured him that would be delightful, laid firmly under her bag the magazine she had been intending to read, and smiled reassuringly across the table at her young companion. At the waiter's suggestion she ordered a chicken sandwich, milk, and deep-dish apple pie.

"Make it two." The corporal thrust back his sandy hair with an awkward gesture and added in a sudden rush of words without looking at her, but drawing on the cloth with his knife, "Look ma'am, I want to get this over. Could I ask you, please—can a man ever break his own engagement?" Then, as if to make his question less personal, "I saw your USO pin, so I knew it would be all right to sort of get your slant."

"Why yes, of course, men have to break their engagements sometimes," said Mrs. Brown, realizing there was much to be said for carrying the USO pin in one's bag instead of wearing it. All her life she had carefully avoided interfering in peoples' private affairs. She had had trouble enough making her own decisions without feeling that she could give advice to other people. Certainly, she never offered any unless explicitly requested.

She ate her meal in silence while the boy across from her talked on about all sorts of ordinary matters. He did not ask for her opinion again. In fact he gave her little real information, merely, that the girl was to meet him in the city that was Mrs. Brown's destination also. "Her name's Adelaide Wait. She said she'd ask the USO where she could get a room." Later he added, "I guess we'll be getting married soon." But his tone only emphasized the reluctance his whole meandering talk had indicated.

Walking back to her berth she wondered what was troubling the boy about his engagement. Her interest made her realize how often USO workers all over the country must have a fleeting glimpse of other peoples' lives, and never any more. Certainly the USO, briefly encountering service personnel as it did, was no sort of work for people who craved to know all of any individual's story. The short contact which was all these transient times usually afforded, required, she knew, both skill and tact and the realization that you might do more harm than good if you intruded sympathy or offered gratuitous advice.

She sighed, thinking of her luncheon companion. Wisdom about the immediate moment was a hard kind of knowledge to come by.

She wondered if she should have made it easier for him to tell her more.

Arriving at her seat Mrs. Brown found the section empty. The woman across the aisle explained that the young mother had gone forward a couple of cars to play bridge with three other girls. "She took a pillow along so she could rig up a bed for Susan."

Gazing out into the growing dusk, Mrs. Brown gave some preliminary thought to the work ahead of her. Though this was her first field trip she had kept in touch with this phase of the work. She knew there were certain standard services the USO aimed to provide wherever there were large concentrations of service personnel. Unzipping her alligator dispatch case, she ran her eye down a list of figures for one large terminal USO covering an eleven month period: 25,883 gallons of coffee served, 501,828 doughnuts, 643,218 sandwiches for a total attendance during that time of slightly over a million men. A footnote added that the woman who made marmalade for that particular snack bar never brought in less than eighteen gallons at one time. There was also the additional housing item of twelve to fifteen thousand applicants per month.

Already Mrs. Brown knew that the bulk of USO service was meeting the individual needs of innumerable people: a sailor who had to know where to buy a cap before the Shore Patrol picked him up as being out of uniform; a young couple asking where they could go for their honeymoon and have a perfectly wonderful time while spending hardly any money; two English boys who had just visited a large American city and now wanted to see something "scenic"—What would the USO suggest?—Perhaps a little boating?; hundreds of servicemen looking for relatives who had no telephones and whose addresses they could only guess at; negotiating a seat in a bomber for a boy on emergency furlough; trying to locate suitable rooms; sewing on buttons and chevrons by the uncounted thousands and not letting the blood from a pricked finger spot the uniform; writing letters home—*Your boy has just been here. We thought you'd like to know he's looking very well.*

Only thousands of volunteers could perform such quantities of small, personal services—only volunteers, Mrs. Brown thought, who found in the USO a channel for their need to help in the war effort. Of course some of these would regard whatever they were doing as the most important matter in a great emergency. Most people, however, kept a fairly good sense of perspective, knowing that such an organization as the USO, even when it functioned at its best, was only one small segment of a tremendous struggle. . . .

Absorbed in her thoughts, she let her fingers shuffle idly through the papers in her lap until one caught her eye and made her smile at the ever-present need for flexibility in such an undertaking. Apparently, there was no being sure ahead of time what the demand would be, even when you thought you had received a perfectly definite order. Before the Infantry Day parade in one large city, this paper noted, the Commanding Officer of 205 jeep drivers who were to bring in 500 Purple Heart men for the ceremonies, asked if the USO could supply his boys with coffee, sandwiches, and doughnuts when they reached the city. The USO said, "Yes of course!" It rounded up the food, only to have it eaten ahead of time by a lusty group of Seabees. Very fast reprovisioning ensued, and the Commanding Officer of the jeeps was so pleased when he arrived that to show his appreciation he said they would all stop in again on their way home from the parade!

Flexibility meant also, Mrs. Brown knew, holding back when additional services you offered were not desired. She had been in a club one night when a sailor, older than the run of boys, unshaven, red-eyed, and dirty from a long train trip, asked for help in finding a new and unlisted telephone number. When it was obtained, he called it on the desk telephone so they could not help hearing part of the conversation. At his end of the line three words were enough, "Honey, I'm home!" The tears rolled unchecked down his cheeks.

When he hung up he said, "Lady, excuse me for breaking. I didn't mean to break that way but I've been gone over two years, and when I heard my wife's voice—well, I didn't mean to break, lady, but I just couldn't help it."

They wrote out directions so he could find the new address, then asked, "Would you like to clean up a little first?"

"No thank you, lady." The tears started again. "That's mighty nice of you but *she* said to hurry and come right home, and that's what I've been dreaming of for over two years so I can't waste any time now it's so near!"

As Mrs. Brown pushed her papers together preparatory to returning them to her dispatch case, a yellow sheet attracted her attention. It was headed, "They Do Appreciate the USO." Picking it up she glanced at a couple of paragraphs: "A soldier came back for a second goodbye before he boarded his train this morning to repeat how grateful he was for the night's rest, a shower, and a shave. 'You know that shaving kit had everything in it a man could want except an orchid and a date!' Then he added, 'I suppose if I ever come through here again you people will have those little items all taken care of too!' "

The other paragraph dealt with a different client: "A sailor stopped at our desk and told us again and again how good our coffee was. Then he asked diffidently, 'Would you mind ma'am, giving me your name and address? Me and my buddies want to write you what it meant to the bunch of us to have a place to shave and take a shower and eat after a hard trip clear across the country. Forty men,' he added, 'and all of us cooks.' "

Arriving at her immediate destination, Mrs. Brown checked her bags and went at once to the USO in the main terminal. Just ahead of her, as the crowd moved toward the central desk, was a group of overseas men still in their combat uniforms. They looked dirty and tired. From their talk she gathered this was their first stop in the country. Suddenly one of them stepped up to a vase of red carnations on the desk. He touched them, smelled them, said, "Oh, good!"

The woman behind the desk smiled at his pleasure.

"Pretty roses, huh!"

She laughed. "Listen, boy, they're still carnations, just as they were before you went away."

He grinned. "Oh, I forgot. Can I have one?"

When she nodded, each man in the group took one. Then forming a chain, they marched through the station singing at the top of their lungs.

Going up to introduce herself, Mrs. Brown heard a sailor inquire if there was a Children's Home where he could spend the week-end. Without asking him why he wanted to, the woman on duty made a telephone call, wrote an address on a piece of paper, and said, "These people will be glad to have you as their guest for the week-end."

"Gosh, thanks, ma'am. You see I was brought up in a Children's Home—thought I'd like to spend my leave talking to the kids and bringing 'em some candy."

From the moment she met her, Mrs. Brown liked the woman in charge, a Mrs. Fielding. Even better, she had the feeling she was herself accepted as a person with whom problems might be frankly discussed. She was grateful for the prestige her new assignment was evidently giving her. Her new friend, a wiry little woman in early middle-age, had energy without oppressive nervous tension and, as Mrs. Brown was to observe over the three day period she was there, an out-going attitude toward people that was sympathetic without being unduly curious.

"Let me show you the Nap Room first," she suggested. "Every bed is taken."

As they went through the crowd, Mrs. Brown remembered it was standard practice to label each napper with a card stating when he must be awakened, and one worker usually had this as her special responsibility. She knew too that there were USO's in a few stations that provided cribs and other infant facilities for servicemen's babies. They were called "bawl-rooms" by the disrespectful.

Following her guide she saw two sailors trying to arrange make-shift beds by pushing chairs and benches together. Mrs. Fielding excused herself to get them pillows and blankets. When she reappeared well loaded, one of the boys sprang up to help her. She made him lie down, take off his shoes for greater comfort, and then propped up his head with a couple of pillows.

Once settled, he lit a cigarette, picked up his magazine, and grinned appreciatively at her. "This is just like home: reading and smoking in bed."

When she tried to fix his friend in the same way, he waved her off. "Don't bother about me. I'll spread out just like I am."

"Oh go on and let her fix you," the first sailor urged him. "Can't you see she's your second mother?"

Mrs. Fielding laughed comfortably and went on, leaving the boy to enjoy himself in the way that best suited him. Then she pointed out to her guest an inconspicuous door labeled Private. "That's a small room we keep for badly wounded men who have to wait between trains. It has an extra wide outside door so that a litter can be carried in if necessary. The Military Police and the Shore Patrol know about it and bring people who need it. Just now a wheel-chair boy is in there with a medical attendant. They are having to wait all day for a Pullman reservation. We're quite proud of the privacy of our sick-bay."

Quietly she opened the main Nap Room door. Mrs. Brown saw her amazed look, and peered over her shoulder. In front of them, running lengthwise of the room, were two long rows of double-decker beds each with posts at the head and foot. Every bed was occupied and on each post up and down the room a shoe was neatly placed, sole up. Mrs. Fielding beckoned to the elderly woman in charge, and the three of them stepped outside the door where they could talk without disturbing the nappers.

"The first boy in tonight was a paratrooper," the attendant explained with a smile in her eyes. "He picked out the bed right in front of the door—guess he was too tired to walk any farther. I stepped out for a moment and when I came back he was sound asleep with his boots on the bedposts. After that every boy followed his example. I didn't have the heart to correct them. I knew they did it because they thought it was the custom here and they were so grateful for a chance to lie down, they wanted to do exactly right!"

As they turned away Mrs. Brown inquired whether they had many requests for rooms both for overnight and for week-ends.

"The demand is simply terrific! We can't take care of more than a third of our requests. I'd like you to look at our housing files when we get back to the main desk. But let's stop at the snack bar a minute since we're near it."

They stood at one side of the counter out of the way while khaki, blue, gray, and white streamed past. Presently a boy with two overseas ribbons approached them.

"Remember me?" he asked Mrs. Fielding though a twitch at the corner of his mouth indicated he knew well enough she would be surprised at the question. "I remember you, ma'am, no kidding!"

Thin steam from his coffee cup rose before grinning blue eyes in a deeply tanned face. "I was on a casualty train that laid over here for several days in July of '41. I heard the C.O. ask you if anything could be done to keep it secret that such a train was in the yards. We were all sick to death of sight-seers. You said, 'Of course,' and you spoke to every station employee!"

"I remember now. And nobody came to stare at you, did they?"

"Not a soul. But the most important thing was that first evening when you and some other women lugged baskets of food down to us."

"That was a trek!" she laughed. "The USO supply room was upstairs then. The Station Master helped us. There were over four hundred of you and the only things we had in sufficient quantity were cookies, candy, and cigarettes. We never were caught that short again."

"Don't worry, ma'am. There was **nothing** wrong with **what you** did for us that night. We hadn't had anything to eat for twelve hours. I never thought a lemon drop could taste so good!"

Later in the day Mrs. Brown was shown the housing cards. She was amazed at the numbers. "Do you mean all these rooms have been checked by personal visit to make sure they are suitable?"

Mrs. Fielding nodded. "Also we telephone before we send anyone out to a listed room to make sure it is still available. Then we give the room hunter a card with the prospective landlady's name and address on it, and ask both parties to report to us if the room is taken. We also make a note of any other matters we think may be relevant."

Mrs. Brown complimented her on such a careful system, and promptly looked up the name WAIT, ADELAIDE. The card indicated that the girl had been referred to a certain room for a two-day reservation. There was also a notation that she had been undecided at first as to whether she wanted a single or a double room, and as to whether she should make the reservation for two days or for a longer period. She might be getting married, she said, but was not sure her fiance would be able to meet her.

"Do you remember this Wait girl?" Mrs. Brown asked when there was a lull and no one was within hearing.

"Yes, I do. She seemed a nice child though I was surprised when she spoke of being married. She was so impersonal about it."

Mrs. Brown reported what she had learned from the boy involved. "He said he consulted me because of my USO pin so I feel a little responsible for him. There doesn't seem to be much enthusiasm on either side for this wedding."

Several weeks later Mrs. Brown received a little, informal report from Mrs. Fielding that both of these young people had come to the USO there for advice. Developments extending over some time and including a case worker in the girl's home town had then revealed that her father, a widower, wished to remarry, but his prospective wife did not want Adelaide to live with them. Her father sincerely believed she was fond of Robert Hudson, with whom she had grown up, and he of her. He had, therefore, promoted the marriage as being a helpful solution all the way around. He had not realized how reluctant both the young people were. Discussion of the whole situation had also brought out the fact that Adelaide had an aunt (her mother's sister) of whom she was very fond who would be only too happy to have the girl live with her. It had not occurred to the father that he could make such a suggestion.

Mrs. Fielding reported that the boy and girl said goodbye in her office. "They seemed to like each other very much—kid fashion."

Many Happy Returns

"We made it!" shouted the boy against the roar and the hissing steam of two freight engines, banked with snow, that had finally brought the troop train into the Junction. "We got through! Boy, what a storm!"

He was just that many words ahead of the crowd. I felt he hadn't said all he meant to. But open flew the doors. In swarmed the men. It was only a medium-sized waiting room but the USO had been serving these troop trains for some months now and we'd learned a thing or two about managing. We'd found out how to set up shop so as to move them fast, and yet not miss a boy. Each fellow had his choice too: cocoa or coffee, egg sandwiches or cookies. If the mob wasn't too great we could give them both.

It wasn't often that I had a chance to pass out food. Mostly, I had to stay by my desk and answer questions, send telegrams for the boys, sew on a button, write a letter breaking an engagement, write a letter proposing. It was as though our way-station at the end of such a long run with another unbroken stretch ahead became in the boys' minds a focal point for taking action.

You learned, when a boy shot simultaneously out of that train and out of hours of mulling over his problem—you learned, when he came to you all worked up for any one of a dozen reasons, to fit your mood to his, even for five minutes, or at least not to mar his mood.

You learned to recognize the signs in their eyes, in their hesitant or keyed-up speech, in the give-away motions of their idle hands. One thing you took for granted—though they were mostly a bunch of fine sports and had a quick laugh handy, and wouldn't take pity from anybody—they were all of them homesick.

"There wasn't a message for me, was there?" The noise outside was not so great now, and, by leaning forward a little over the desk, my first visitor, who had not joined the surge toward food, could make me hear without shouting. For just a moment he looked squarely at me. "My name's Charlie Matthews."

But I knew his name. I knew it the instant he gave me that one brief glance. "You'll be waiting here an hour," I stalled. "Perhaps you will get it. Why not have a snack?"

"Sure," he said and walked slowly to a counter.

It was Charlie Matthew's nineteenth birthday. Under my desk blotter was a telegram from his mother asking us to have a birthday cake with candles for him. We often provided birthday cakes, like every USO, and we'd have had Charlie's ready for him on my desk, except for the storm.

I had ordered it the minute the wire came. In fact my 'phone call about it to Mrs. Nordstrom whose turn it was to bake, was about the last call over the wires before the storm hit. And such drifts! But this morning, the wind had dropped, dead calm, and the sun shone on a white and sparkling world.

All our volunteers beyond the village were snowed in. But we had six or eight stand-bys near the station. I got word around to them any way I could, because all the telephone wires were down.

I had intended to be quite matter-of-fact in explaining to Charlie so as not to increase his homesickness, but when he looked at me so straight and I saw he'd thought of the possibility that he would be remembered as his buddies no doubt had been in other places, something made me stall for time.

But what was the use, I asked myself, as I answered questions and made notes of errands to be done later for the boys. In a free moment I glanced out of the window toward the snowbound mountains. Mrs. Nordstrom in her neat farmhouse two valleys to the north might as well be in Norway.

"Gracious . . ." I thought suddenly, "I must really be getting as overtired as they're always telling me. Specks in my eyes and moving specks at that." I blinked, saw the snowglare against my lids, and looked again.

That was no speck. That was somebody coming down the trail and only the Nordstroms lived that way.

Then I knew as sure as I knew the USO had never fallen down on a birthday before, that we weren't falling down on this one. That was Mrs. Nordstrom on her skis. What if that was the trickiest trail for miles around? What if she wasn't as young as she once was? Mrs. Nordstrom had never failed us yet, and this wasn't going to be her first time. I knew her poles were tucked under her arm and that in her hands was a square cardboard box.

I'd let her make that sharpest curve. I looked at my watch. Twenty minutes before the train was due to leave. They could eat the cake on the train. The thing was to get it to Charlie, to tell him, "Your mother ordered it and here it is."

I'd speak to the Commanding Officer. Maybe he wouldn't make the boys go aboard ahead of time. Then I let myself look at the mountain again. Of course she'd made the curve!

The C.O. was a swell, fatherly sort of soul. "Suppose we line the men up facing where she'll come in," he said. "Then when you hand Matthews the telegram, it'll be the signal for them to start singing."

So that's the way it was. There was a little rise in the ground not far beyond the village. I figured when I saw her skim over that as she went into the lower trail and out of sight, that I'd count ten and give the signal. That ought to bring her in just right.

I saw her. I counted ten but what I was really saying was, "Oh pray God she may not fall down and spill it." I hardly realized I'd handed Charlie the telegram until such a vigorous and male "Happy birthday to you" hit the air that I jumped. The boys were putting all they had into it.

But where was Mrs. Nordstrom? She didn't come. She must have stopped. Didn't she realize they were waiting? Hadn't she seen them all lined up?

I saw the C.O. turn his head quickly toward me. Distinctly, through an awful sense of panic, I heard those voices coming to the end, "Happy birthday, Charlie M—"

And then serenely around the final curve came Mrs. Nordstrom holding steadily in front of her a square white birthday cake with nineteen lighted candles.

CHAPTER II

Come Saturday

It was early evening, the time of night when families would normally be washing the supper dishes, preparatory to a leisurely evening. After a busy day homes would be coming into their own, places where members of the family could let down and do as they pleased individually, or join in whatever household activities might be afoot.

But these were not normal times and the men pouring out of one of the country's large training camps with Saturday evening leave had no homes of their own accessible. They had for the evening only what the nearby town afforded. It was a medium-sized place, some 50,000 inhabitants counting men, women, and children. The camp had 75,000, all men, all young. Those who were off-duty tonight were "on the town." The community, through no choice of its own, was host.

The stream of khaki pouring into town by truck, car, and foot would fill the movie houses without noticeably lessening its volume, and would pack the eating places. Stores would be crowded to capacity, some private homes would have soldier guests. The rest—the bulk—would be GIs at large.

Four clubs operated by the member Agencies of the USO had been set up in the community to help give these men some sort of substitute for home. Effort was made to provide the man on leave with facilities for doing what he might like to do by himself or with a few others: desks and materials for writing letters, dark rooms for developing films, the newest magazines, symphonic recordings, bowling, pool, etc. Effort was also made to have general programs under way in the clubs which he would be welcome to join: dancing, dramatics, classes in all sorts of subjects from languages to radio script writing, singing, crafts, discussion groups.

The largest USO in town was housed in a big recreation building erected by the Federal Government for the purpose. Three of the six USO Agencies ran this place together, one director being in charge with the other Agency representatives functioning as his associates. Each of these professional staff workers was paid directly by his own Agency which was then reimbursed by the National USO. Dances on a large scale were the most conspicuous feature of this club though many other activities with capacity attendance were carried on simultaneously in other parts of the building.

Down the street, a couple of blocks from this Federal Recreation Building, was another USO club, housed in a neat frame structure formerly used by a church. This was very much a family club, and much attention was paid to music and to games.

Half-a-mile in the opposite direction, a two-story warehouse had been made into a third club. Here there was no dancing, but every other interest of servicemen had been energetically provided for. If headline activities could have been chosen from so many, they would have been the extensive and varied snack bar and the equipment available to men who wished to make things requiring complicated and power-driven tools.

In another part of the city was an old, rambling residence in front of which still another USO sign swung in the wind, a much-used Agency center that had been swamped far beyond its equipment ever since military activities had first impinged upon the town. In charge for a year now was a young woman of unusual capacity, but even her resourcefulness could not enlarge the square-footage of these cramped quarters or make efficient the poor arrangement of the lower floor. For some time she had been wondering if the sensible course would not be to move this club bodily into the Federal Recreation Building. Two reasons for such a change impressed her. There would be ample room there for the type of activities in which her club specialized. And, in the second place, she felt the interests of women and girls might receive more adequate consideration in the whole USO set-up of the town if her Agency joined the three men's Agencies now working there.

Morning

This Saturday had started soon after six for Mr. Redfield, director of the USO in the recreation building, when the 'phone beside his bed had rung and a young, nasal voice had shouted, "Hi, Red! This is Butch—*you* know—plays the sax. We're pulling out in thirty minutes. Thought you might want to see us off." Dead as he was, being now past fifty and having crawled into bed at two a.m. when the club had finally become comparatively quiet for the night, Mr. Redfield felt a recurrence of the pleased surprise that had come to him rather often these last months—a surprise that young men should warm up to him. What rather limited sense of humor he had told him that they must be pretty desperate for human companionship to go in for calling him "Red" and for making any point at all of having him around for any purpose except management and administration. They probably just assumed in the rush and general dislocation of their lives that he was another of the hail-fellow-well-met club directors, which he had never even tried to be, knowing that such a role was completely beyond him.

Never a warm person, the blatant emotionalism of the war had sent him even deeper into his shell. Occasionally, however, when some boy "counted him in," as did this youngster, he prayed an almost desperate prayer that he might make the right motions in response. So now he tried to shake himself awake and clear the night's huskiness out of his throat enough to give this telephoning soldier the right answer.

"You bet I want to see you off." Both energy and interest were called for so he repeated a heartier, "You bet!" and added, reaching for his clothes while the 'phone was still in his hand, "See you any minute now."

He did hope the boy wouldn't expect him to pray in public. The mere thought made him feel suddenly constricted. He couldn't do it—not out there on the platform. With Mr. Redfield spiritual convictions went so deep that it was beyond him to talk about them. Often he felt he was no sort of person to represent a religious Agency. He had made that as clear as he could to his national office. They had seemed to understand his halting explanations and had assured him that his qualifications as a whole were satisfactory. Together they had planned that all religious work should be handled by one of his associates—a man who was only too glad to take on this responsibility.

Mr. Redfield sometimes thought this associate of his must have a sixth sense for knowing when boys had something on their minds they wanted to discuss. Any number of times he had heard him say, "I'll tell the Chaplain you'll be in to see him," and had seen the boy's relieved expression at the thought that the ice would be broken for him. Often on these occasions Mr. Redfield had said to himself that he wouldn't have known the man was worried.

He had to push his mind this morning, whipping it on to think of the arrangements he ought to make before leaving the club. You could never tell when these troop trains would actually get under way. Even his automatic, early morning planning creaked. He must be slipping. He used to be able to get along on four hours sleep and think nothing of it. Shoving his wallet into his pocket, thrusting his arms into his coat, he picked up his hat, and sternly pulled himself together. Who was he to pay any attention to being tired? This week boys had hiked across France—sleeping where, and for how long? With such a break-through they had gone ahead on nerve and will power. The least he could do—

Then he was in his car, the wind cool and refreshing in his face. A cop seeing his USO sticker and guessing that he was headed for the terminal, waved him through a red light. There he was at last, geared again to his waking life in which, thank heaven, he had no time to consider himself as an individual. Now there was only the war, and his part in the total effort, the USO.

To everybody's surprise the train left practically on time and Butch presented no problem at all. What he wanted was a crushing handshake, somebody to grin at and slap on the back. Then with a "Be seein' you, Red," his heavy Army boots made for the train steps. Halfway up, he was stopped by a soldier coming down. They exchanged a word, then Butch pointed out his friend on the platform and yelled down to him, "Say, Red, here's a guy wants you to do something for him."

Mr. Redfield hurried over to the steps, an anxious look in his eyes, put there by fear lest he might not be able to do everything possible for any one of these men who fortunately didn't know as well as he did what they were headed for. Just then came a roar of gruff orders, MPs appeared out of the earth, and Mr. Redfield found himself reaching under the arm of one to seize a twenty dollar bill that Butch's friend was frantically trying to get to him. Clipped to it, he saw, was a short list of names.

"Send 'em all flowers for me," the boy yelled over the MP's head as he hurried up the train steps. "They all live in Kansas City. You can get the addresses out of a telephone book some place."

"I'll attend to it," Mr. Redfield shouted back.

As he parked his car in the club driveway one of the staff opened the window and called, "Telephone, Mr. Redfield. Can't get her to leave a message."

Before he had a chance to say more than Hello such a flood of belligerency poured into his ear that it was clear the woman at the other end of the line expected a No to whatever request she was about to make. Then it came: she and her friends wanted to use the USO auditorium for a good old-fashioned revival meeting.

As pleasantly as he could Mr. Redfield told her that since Catholics, Protestants, and Jews were co-operating in USO work, it was the policy not to hold religious meetings as such in the clubs where other facilities—such as churches, town halls and so forth—were available.

"No religion in USO clubs?" came back the voice unmistakably tinged with tight-lipped fanaticism.

"Oh, plenty of religion." This one was easy even for the reserved Mr. Redfield. "Music, hymn singing that all the faiths can take part in, religious literature always to be had for the taking." He did not add, as he might have, that even when the racks were put in inconspicuous places, it was impressive how rapidly the supply dwindled. "And local Protestant ministers, rabbis, and priests are generous about coming to the club so as to be available if any of the men want to consult them."

"How about the Catholics?" insisted the voice. "I heard——."

"In communities predominantly Protestant where there are no Catholic churches for the Catholic servicemen to attend, communion breakfasts are sometimes arranged in USO clubs following mass held in a nearby camp or in the church of a neighboring town."

"And the Jews?"

"Their High Holy Days are very seldom celebrated in clubs. Occasionally a USO club loans its facilities just as individual Christian churches have."

"What about the Protestants? Do they have any chance at all?"

"There are Java Club meetings Sunday mornings and vespers Sunday afternoon. Announcement is made of all religious services being held in the town. Free transportation is provided to all places of worship for men who wish to go—"

"Too easy!" the voice pronounced judgment and rang off.

"Too easy!" thought Mr. Redfield swept by a sudden wave of anger, though he knew he should not be so provoked by his cross-questioner. He glanced at his watch, saw it was nearly time for the members of the staff to begin coming in for informal discussion and reporting, as they did almost daily between regularly scheduled staff conferences, and hailed the stooped and white-haired janitor who happened to be passing his office door. "Oh, Mr. Brown, if you have a chance will you bring me some coffee and toast? I can't very well leave the office right now."

"Too easy, indeed," repeated Mr. Redfield. It would be hard to think of anything more difficult. Theoretically the three faiths had co-operated before, but their work in the USO was the first time in the history of the world that Jews, Catholics, and Protestants as religion-ists had together not only made plans, but budgeted for them, and then carried them out in practical day-by-day work. Proselytizing, ruled out at the start, had not marred the picture. But it had been inevitable that institutional vested interests would sometimes collide in the USO as well as in the world at large and that even where there was the best possible spirit, certain concepts of one faith or another would make the actual business of co-operation difficult. Even the matter of having religious literature available had not been simple to arrange. The problem was resolved now by having Agency-con-ducted clubs, whether Protestant, Catholic, or Jewish, display three identical racks for the literature of the three faiths. No, it had been far from easy. However, in his private opinion, something funda-mental to a religious world had been made richer.

The rest of the morning went by, devoid of a sense of time. Respon-sibilities overlapped, doubled up, demanded simultaneous attention. The business aspects alone of running so large a club were time-consuming. One of the building men reported they were now han-dling a hundred cases of coca-cola daily, that the postage sales to servicemen for the past month, in spite of franking privileges, had run well over $5,000, that four to five thousand dollars worth of tele-phoning was done every month. Keeping the club decently clean was getting to be a major problem and the laundry was slower and slower on deliveries.

"We'll have to close the swimming pool tonight," the Athletics director reported. "Haven't got a towel in the place."

"Towels?" repeated a volunteer who had just come into the main office to put a soldier's discharge money into the safe for him. "He'll come for this Monday," she interpolated. "It's clearly marked with his name and number. About towels—I think we can get some for you."

"Bathtowels? So the swimming pool needn't be closed?"

She nodded. Her daughter, she explained, was president of the sixth grade and the whole class was looking for jobs to help the war along. She knew they'd love to start right off on a house-to-house canvass— one bathtowel from every family for the USO.

"Excuse me, Mr. Redfield," a volunteer he didn't know appeared at the door. "The fourth golf club has just called in to report how many servicemen-guests they can accommodate this week-end."

"Miss Rice takes care of that. The number has to be relayed on an equitable basis to all the USOs in town."

"Miss Rice is not in. I'll take a whack at it."

He smiled his thanks as an Army Special Service officer came in the door, swallowing his fervent wish that when volunteers could not keep to their regular schedule, they would get substitutes. It was ticklish business keeping the golf arrangements straightened out and this woman's airy use of the word "whack" made him uneasy.

"Good morning, Captain."

The assistant cashier interrupted them. "Will you just O.K. these six bills, Mr. Redfield? I've checked the invoices item by item. And please initial this petty cash check. They need more wrapping paper and string for doing up the boys' gifts tonight. Thank you, sir. Excuse me, Captain."

The Captain was affable but whether by nature or for diplomatic reasons, Mr. Redfield wasn't sure. Certainly he had rather large orders on his mind. Mr. Redfield was used to arranging the weekly Army broadcast from the USO auditorium for him—had the next program well in mind already, in fact. But he hadn't expected a requisition for Junior Hostesses this week for a dance on the post.

"These girls are dancing their slippers to shreds," he demurred. "We've a big party on tonight. Sunday's an awfully heavy day for them with games and musical stuff here at the club. Then to go out to the post again Monday night—You need three hundred?"

"Look," said the Captain with sudden earnestness, "It's special. Let the girls off Sunday and send them out to us instead."

Mr. Redfield understood. Men shipping out. Men and men and men being rushed into the great break-through in France. If they wanted a dance the last night, the girls would be there. "You bet, Captain."

While the Captain thanked him and said goodbye Mr. Redfield remembered that he must check over the list of Junior Hostesses for tonight and be sure the committee had been scrupulously fair to young women of all religious backgrounds. All creeds must be duly represented in the hostesses as they would be in the guests.

Afternoon

Shrilly the noon whistles blew. He must hurry and drop in on the meeting the Information Committee was holding. Their whole set-up needed to be refocused to take care of the men returning from overseas.

"The scrap leather situation is really something," said a nervous voice behind him as he started across the lobby to the meeting.

He turned with friendly interest for, nervous or not, this specialist on his staff was a great comfort to him. She seemed to recognize a truth he felt to be terribly important—that peoples' lives were all of a piece, not a series of wholly disconnected interests. Her attitude towards crafts for servicemen and women was that tempting tools

and materials should be available right in the midst of other club activities—not off in a corner by themselves. It seemed to work. He had
seen men sprawled at a table on the edge of the dance floor doing
leatherwork who would never have bothered to hunt up a separate
crafts room. They liked to be in the midst of things, a relaxed foot
keeping time with the music.

"I'm trying the shoe factories," she said. "We'll have to cut our
product to the leather scraps."

But of course they both knew, he thought, walking on, that you
couldn't carry that idea too far. Real camera fiends wanted a dark
room to work in where they wouldn't be disturbed. Electric kilns for
drying small knickknacks had to have special space and even noisy
sawing and hammering jobs required their own workshop. In still
another room the men were doing beautiful things with plastics.

He thrust his hand in his inside coat pocket and pulled out the
plastic cigarette case a snub-nosed Marine had given him. But all he'd
done for the kid was let him talk one day when he had an awful
grouch on. He'd seen a horrible thing with a bulldozer once. He had
described it four times during the hour he had talked. Seemed to have
to keep pushing it angrily out of his mind.

Putting the cigarette case back his fingers touched a bill. He pulled
it out and remembered the Kansas City flowers. This would be a fine
job for the Personal Services Committee. He went out into the main
lobby where three flat-topped desks pushed end-to-end handled individual requests for special jobs. The volunteers on duty explained to
him that they were just clearing up last night's requests.

One of them was laughing as he approached. "Goat's milk," she
said to him. "Do you know how much it is a quart? Well, neither
did we. But last night a cadaverous looking GI asked us. He looked
like a PW and we thought some doctor had prescribed goat's milk
for him. So we said we'd find out. We called—how many places was
it?—thirteen, before we found a dairy that handled it. Then we had
the soldier paged and when he turned up we informed him with

some considerable satisfaction in our efficiency about what the cost per day would be to him. 'Oh,' he said in mild surprise, 'Thank you, ma'am, but you shouldn't have bothered. I didn't want to drink it. Just was thinking of starting a goat farm and wondered if it'd pay!' "

The Kansas City job was too simple to make much impression on them. They had corralled telephone books from all over the country and they would set some helper to looking up the addresses. "But this assignment we're just finishing now was a woman-sized job!".

Mr. Redfield asked for particulars and was told that a well-worn bundle had been brought into the club by a chaplain. When they opened it they found over 200 scraps of paper: pieces of paper bags, backs of cigarette packages, odds and ends. On every piece was a lot of close writing and an address—each scrap a letter home. With them was a message to the USO from a Marine Colonel, C.O. on one of the recently taken Pacific islands, asking that the scraps be put in envelopes and mailed to the persons specified on each. "We are sending the farthest away ones, airmail. The three of us here happened to have some extra airmail stamps in our handbags and it seemed a good idea."

A Junior Hostess was waiting to speak to him. "Mr. Redfield, there's a sailor in the lounge who wants to talk to you. He doesn't know your name but he wants to see the 'head man.' He's not in a very sunshiny mood."

Mr. Redfield said goodbye to the Committee and started in search of the sailor. How thankful he was for the way this Personal Services set-up was working out. It was a perfect job for volunteers—they simply received the requests and took care of them. He was so grateful not to have any responsibility in the matter. "I'm no good at 'inspiring' volunteers," he said under his breath as he went down the hall.

Back in the lobby the three women, who found their job absorbing but far from simple, knew from their own experience that all volunteers worth their salt were self-starters if they were given scope and the whole responsibility.

"Hello, son," Mr. Redfield said to the sailor who was sitting legs apart, elbows on knees, his drooping head clasped between his hands. "I heard you were asking for me. Come along and have a sandwich and a cup of coffee. Seems to me it's been a long time since breakfast."

At the Snack Bar Mr. Redfield ordered for both of them when his companion showed no interest. Chicken salad sandwiches were the specialty today and while a young woman with white hair spread them he observed that this was the day when the Snack Bar was in charge of seven women all of whom had lost men on Bataan. They had been working together for a good many months now.

Mr. Redfield carried a tray with their sandwiches and coffee to a little table where they could talk without being overheard. It was the dull hour between lunch and afternoon snacks.

"My wife's left me," the sailor suddenly blurted out, his tone bracing him, Mr. Redfield felt, against advice from the "head man."

Mr. Redfield went on eating his sandwich without comment. Knowing nothing about the situation he couldn't honestly say either, "That's too bad," or "That's good but—" Better let the man get it off his chest. It was a rambling story of a war marriage, the woman evidently a good deal older than he was. As he talked on and on Mr. Redfield saw he was even younger than he had thought at first. The relief of talking the thing out was giving him more of a grip on himself. He sat up straighter and when he finally said, "She could go for all me but I wanted a kid and she didn't," he looked Mr. Redfield straight in the eye. "I just love kids," he added.

Suddenly Mr. Redfield glanced at his watch as though he had just remembered something. "Look here, sailor, have you got time to lend me a hand?" With a suggestion of emergency in his voice he explained about the bathtowels for the swimming pool and the sixth-graders. "The woman who started them off on this canvass called in awhile ago to say they were having great success and could we have a little celebration for them when they arrive here which ought to be almost any minute now. Of course we'll give them some ice-cream but what could we do that they'd like for a little ceremony?"

The sudden interest in the sailor's eyes was good to see. "I'll tell you what, mister. I'll get four or five of my buddies—they're in there playing pool. And when the kids get here, we'll pipe them aboard like they were officers, line them up, collect their towels, and then do a hornpipe for them. We're pretty good—three of us—no fooling. Then we can dish out the food. They'll like that fine—being entertained by real live sailors."

Thankful to have two matters thus taken care of at once, Mr. Redfield hurried back to his office by way of the Home Hospitality desk. The staff worker in charge told him there was a steady stream of requests for overnight or week-end lodging with private families. Some men expressed a preference for Catholic or for Jewish or for Protestant hosts. Others were indifferent. And the same attitudes were true of people who opened their homes to servicemen. Lately she had tried matching up hosts and guests according to hobbies and had heard of some combinations that had worked very well indeed. "One man—you know, Mr. Larrabee out on Lakewood Drive—was a little reluctant to offer his saddlehorses to GI guests. But a dashing young sergeant whom I sent out there the other day prevailed upon him to let him ride his prize hunter. It seems the sergeant was a headline polo player and that first afternoon his horsemanship saved a child's life in a runaway. Now Mr. Larrabee says, 'He can ride any horse I have!' "

There was a small, early supper scheduled for that evening in one of the dressing rooms just off the auditorium stage, almost the only spot in the big building that wouldn't be monopolized by milling servicemen from seven o'clock on. It was a meeting of the Forum Committee, six or eight men and women who lived in the town. They had been insistent that he join them. These people had run one series of forums with great success. Not that the attendance had been large but the discussion afterwards had been vigorous and, on the whole, both intelligent and forward-looking. The committee was keen to get further plans in the works and was meeting tonight to decide what topics should be discussed.

Perhaps now, Mr. Redfield thought, if he closed his office door he might get a few minutes to collect his thoughts in case these people asked him for suggestions. He was in the act of hitching his chair closer to the desk so he could jot down a note or two when the door was flung open so violently it banged against the wall. A very young Marine stood in the doorway, feet wide apart and said belligerently, "Give me a Bible, mister."

Mr. Redfield handed him one of the New Testaments that were always available to servicemen.

"No, not that. I said a Bible—a whole Bible."

Mr. Redfield turned back to search the shelves, but could not immediately lay his hands on one.

"Just like a Christian, never knowing where anything important is!"

His high-keyed petulance was so obviously caused by something else that Mr. Redfield made no attempt to reply and did not turn around until he was sure there was no complete Bible in his office. Then he saw the boy was crying in a tense, grimacing sort of way.

"What did you want with it, son?"

"I wanted you to explain something. The Bible says if your right hand offends you, you ought to cut it off."

Mr. Redfield was momentarily relieved. "That's in the New Testament. I'll find it for you."

The boy took the opened Testament and slowly read the whole chapter. Then he looked up at the Director. "Would you please tell me, sir, does it really mean I should cut my hand off?"

Mr. Redfield assured him it did not and found a Commentary to reassure the boy still further.

"Gosh!" breathed the young Marine and the way he suddenly let his body sprawl in the armchair before the Director's desk showed his relief.

Presently he sat up straighter and leaning forward began telling Mr. Redfield what had been on his mind for a good many months. Back at high school, he and his best friend had gone upstairs one afternoon to his bedroom window and killed sparrows in nearby bushes with a 22 rifle. That evening the body of a man, well known in their community, was found near the same bushes. Neither boy knew who had fired the fatal shot.

For half-an-hour the boy went on talking, his tension decreasing all the while. It was as though relief had released a flood of talk about familiar things—his home, school, friends and run-of-the-day interests bottled up by an anxiety now removed.

Mr. Redfield, listening, was amazed at himself for being involved in a situation of this sort. If he had had any warning he would have called in a religious adviser. But the boy had cornered him with a childish question, he had answered it, and the boy was now doing the rest himself.

"Well, goodbye, sir. I gotta go. It's sure a big help to understand the Bible right."

With an agreeable feeling of increased self-respect—for apparently he hadn't conspicuously failed to meet the boy's need—Mr. Redfield hurried off to the Forum Committee. Returning the friendly greetings of the members, he pulled out the chair saved for him on one side of a card table and sat down to something savory and steaming in a casserole.

The hour he spent with them was a restful interval in a day involved beyond the average. These were fine people, men and women of mature judgment and common sense. One could relax completely with them. The only thing that had begun to trouble him before he was summoned by a staff aide for some special problem out in front, was their enthusiasm for relying on what they called "conversational pickups" for forum subjects. This method of getting a line on interesting topics from what service personnel themselves talked about, might be sound procedure for professional workers trained in group-work techniques. But he was somehow a little fearful about it in the hands of these community leaders.

Evening

The emergency out-front proved to be an older soldier drunk to the point of sobbing. Mr. Redfield spoke to a member of the USO Council who was just coming in the door, a Mr. Davis, and, one of them on either side, they got the soldier into a little side room and onto a cot.

"I'll take over for the time-being," offered Mr. Davis. "You'll be needed out there, Redfield." As a volunteer of long standing he was glad to be useful.

Mr. Redfield thanked him and Mr. Davis sat down to watch developments. The soldier lay quiet. Probably he'd drop off to sleep in a few minutes. Mr. Davis made himself as comfortable as he could on a straight chair, reflecting that drunkenness was really quite a problem for USO clubs. No explicit policy for the country as a whole had ever been suggested, so far as he knew. Anyway different communities would handle the same problem differently no matter what anybody said. Such an emergency organization as the USO was bound to reflect the attitudes, customs, and points of view of the place where a given club was located. On this one question of drink he knew there was plenty of variation. Liquor of course was not sold in USO clubs—that was a definite rule. And he had stood outside the door of USO swingshift dances and seen couples from nearby factories "frisked" for bottles. The attendants had even looked into the girls' handbags to make sure that nothing to drink was taken into the party.

But the question as to whether a club would admit a man already intoxicated was another matter. He remembered a youngster, a paratrooper—one of the nicest faces he'd ever seen—seating himself with great care in one of the lounge chairs and saying to the Senior Hostess who approached him, "I know this is a USO club, ma'am. And I know I've had too much to drink. But may I please sit here quietly and get over it?"

Mr. Davis was perfectly aware, however, that they were not all as quiet or as reasonable as this boy. He knew too that USO standards had to be kept on a high plane unless the organization wanted to go completely out of business.

Two contrasting incidents came to his mind as he sat beside the cot waiting to be sure the fellow was asleep. One had occurred in a distant city when a couple of Marines went by taxi to every USO in town trying to find a place where a young soldier whom they had found in the grass of a vacant lot, could sleep it off. But it was a Saturday night. There were "nice" girls at all the parties and those in charge had not wanted the unconscious man brought in.

In the other case the man himself—a sailor—had taken the initiative. Just off his ship in a strange port, he had asked his way to Main Street, meaning to get to the center of town. But Main Street in that city was far on one side of a growing metropolitan area and proved to be lined with shows of questionable flavor and tawdry cafes.

Starting on his second drink the sailor knew suddenly that the first one had been doped. While he still had his senses about him he got to the door, into the open air, and hailed a passing cab. "Take me to a USO," he told the driver and as the door slammed, passed out cold on the back seat.

The taxi driver took him to a USO and asked for the director. "I wouldn't be surprised if this kid had some cash on him. Doped, evidently. Better sober him up and see."

The club had a Quiet Room and in there they worked on the sailor for a long time. When he finally came around he told them he was on his way to be married, that he had saved up $3500 which he had on him in cash.

Mr. Davis, recalling the incident, was conscious of a warm glow of satisfaction that the sailor had counted on "*a* USO" in an emergency, as though it were a standard brand of help.

The man on the cot was breathing more quietly. Mr. Davis decided to slip out and see if he could find a substitute to keep an eye on him. If possible, he wanted to make a tour of the clubs tonight. A committee of which he was chairman was due to make a report soon and he wanted to see first-hand how things were going. Mr. Cohen, also a Council member, volunteered to do anything he could when he saw Mr. Davis emerge from the room.

"Maybe he has something on his mind. I'll look in now and then and be available if he should want to get something off his chest when he wakes up."

Presently Mr. Davis left the club and walked toward the USO that was housed in a building formerly used by a church. A man's pace on the streets tonight was set by the crowd and the two-way traffic on the sidewalks had extended over into the street itself.

What a mob! Good-natured, orderly as far as he could see, men off duty for the evening or the week-end. Though the town was officially dimmed out there was light enough for him to distinguish the men individually as they passed. In spite of similarity of uniform, it was not hard to guess at differences in background, in education, in social experience. And his ear, keen to variations of accent and of idiom in the steady stream of talking, laughing, griping men, told him that the country as a whole was pretty well represented here tonight.

If the town survived, he thought, as of course it would, though it could never be the same again, the townspeoples' social vision ought to be stretched considerably. This experience, repeated all over the country, should have its healthy aspects. America, gigantic in size and power, was studded with provincialism in its big cities as well as in its villages and towns. If her size and power and influence were to be most richly used in the post-war years the people would have to feel and think as citizens of the country as a whole, not merely as residents of such and such a county or state. Along this line there could not help but be education in the USO experience. Though he and other hosts and hostesses in the clubs might never budge outside their towns, the men who came to them were almost all "outsiders"— "foreigners," he guessed some places were calling them. And in the same way his sons and his friends' sons and daughters, too, were sampling other, distant communities.

With a stream of men going the same way, he turned onto the walk leading up to the former church building. This was a place he always liked to come to. The club itself was apt to be a little mussy—not actually dirty, but newspapers, flung down on davenports, stayed there for awhile, ash trays went unemptied longer than in some other clubs, and frequently a soldier or sailor swung his overcoat across the back of a chair without being made to feel that he must check it before he slumped down comfortably with a magazine.

"Good evening, Mr. Davis!" It was one of the staff who greeted him perfectly cordially but not in such a way as to make him feel the inspector that actually he supposed he was. It was more as though he were a neighbor dropping in. He looked around at the milling crowd and sensed that the boys felt that way about it too. It was a family sort of place. At one end of the long living room some sprightly elderly people sat comfortably in rocking chairs while they talked to little knots of servicemen. In the game room on the other side of the wide lobby, youngsters in their early teens were howling over comic books which they shared noisily with boys in uniform, not many years their seniors.

Nowhere was there any sense of strain, any excessive hovering. Yet somehow you felt "wanted" as even he could tell though the club was run by an Agency not of his faith. For the boys whose faith it was, the "accustomedness" must be especially reassuring.

Table games were being played all over the place tonight. He learned from interested spectators that one game of Monopoly had already been in progress several hours. He heard eager, teasing talk of prizes—shopping certificates offered by various storekeepers in the town, and a first prize of flowers-to-be-telegraphed anywhere, the regular Saturday night contribution of the local florists' association. Farther on, he watched the final hand of what had evidently been a tense rubber of bridge. While they waited to change partners with another table, they amused themselves with the uncomplicated business of standing dominoes on end and by tipping the last in line, knocking over as many as they could. "Nitwits!" growled a lone soldier watching them.

As he continued his stroll about the place, Mr. Davis heard preoccupied people whistling softly in the dark room where they were evidently developing or printing pictures, judging by the acrid smell of chemicals that drifted faintly into the main lounge. In the kitchen a middle-aged couple—a corporal and his wife—were popping corn.

Mr. Davis found that he himself was feeling very much at home. With pleasure he accepted a glass of cold milk offered him by the snack bar attendant. As he leaned one elbow on the counter and drank it slowly he recalled an incident told him by the woman staff worker here. She had said that one day a young sailor, due to ship out shortly, had telegraphed his wife to join him without even trying to find overnight lodging for her in advance. At that time the housing load was so great that not many more than half the people applying for rooms were being taken care of.

Nonetheless, when his wife reached town around midnight, he brought her at once to this club and asked if a room could be found. The woman staff worker called twenty-seven places without success. Then she said rather sharply to the sailor, "*Why* did you telegraph your wife to come? You've been stationed here long enough to know the housing situation is impossible."

She told Mr. Davis in reporting the incident, that the sailor had looked straight at her then with a queer little pitying smile. "It's you

I'm sorry for, lady," he said slowly, "because you've never loved any-body enough to know what it means to have them with you—even for an hour—before you ship out to you-don't-know-where."

Mr. Davis could see why she then gave the couple her own room and slept herself on a couple of the club chairs pushed together.

Walking west he passed a fine old mansion where, on the lower floor, some of the thousands of USO Scrapbooks were being prepared by resourceful volunteers for distribution to the Army, the Navy, Mobile Service, and Overseas Clubs.

Turning into the main street he went on to the center of town where a USO in a renovated warehouse was doing a big Saturday night business. This was the only USO in the community that stayed open all Saturday night. When it had become evident that such a plan was desirable, volunteers had been called for to man the information desk from midnight until 4 a. m. The first to offer her services had been a young woman who worked the other six nights a week in a small war plant.

Tonight he could see the snack bar was doing a terrific business, loaded with food donated by all sorts of organizations. There was a solid line along the counter all the time and much cheerful talk. In the large rooms beyond, games were in progress and on a stage in one of them some amateur show business was going forward with loud encouragement from the audience.

Downstairs small electric machinery was running full tilt. Costume jewelry was evidently a favorite product. He stopped to watch a burly sailor working on a wide, gold wedding ring. Beside him, with a tense frown on his face, was the town's best jeweler as concentrated as the sailor on the design of the engraving. Farther on a Marine, wearing asbestos gloves, was shaping plastic from a discarded juke-box into a fruit bowl on a wooden stand.

By the time he got back to the game room a complete transforma-tion had taken place. Nothing was to be seen on the tables except checkers. There must have been at least fifty intent servicemen bent over the boards. Going almost on a dead run from board to board was a dapper little man who guaranteed to play—and beat—them all.

"Why don't you sit down while you watch?" suggested a sweet little lady pushing a folding chair before her. He thanked her but remained standing, watching her rather than the checker games. Unobtrusively she was looking out for people. A boy with a bandaged leg needed a footstool to rest his heel on. The bulb of a reading lamp burned out with a vivid flare of light and she immediately brought another. But when she came in with a white wicker tray of red apples, she became the center of an eager, jostling mob.

As he went out the side door and started to walk away, the light from a basement window caught his attention. Glancing in, he saw half a dozen hot and earnest musicians—a piano, a violin, two trumpets and a couple of guitars and a small mixed choir—absorbed in learning their parts in what sounded, at that stage of progress, like a very complicated score. What did the end-result matter, since participation was obviously so satisfying to everyone engaged!

Approaching the street corner, Mr. Davis was trying to decide whether he had better walk to the next club or take a bus when a car slowed down to the curb and a woman called to him:

"Going uptown, Mr. Davis? I've a box of cookies to deliver to Miss Sullivan."

It was Mrs. Shaw, a fellow Council member. He was delighted to accept. "This is great luck for me! I was headed for Miss Sullivan's club myself."

"I'm tired clear into the future," announced his chauffeur cheerfully as they went slowly toward their destination in deference both to the war-time speed limit and to the treacherous dim-out.

Mr. Davis was surprised by an admission of weariness from the woman beside him. Ever since he could remember she had been in some sort of useful work in the town. In fact, had the question been put to him, he would unhesitatingly have named her as the most capable and most amiable woman in community activities.

"I think it's because I feel so foiled in this organization of ours. In Council meetings we are always being asked by the professional staff members to make suggestions. We are told again and again that we have much responsibility. And I think we'd all agree that nobody could be treated with greater courtesy than we are by most members of the staff. But somehow when it comes to policy-making decisions, we seem to be told about them, rather than asked to help work them out in the first place. Even with the best will in the world you do often feel like a fifth wheel. Of course if the job gets done, that's what primarily matters and on the whole I think a good job does get done. What do you think about all this?"

Mr. Davis laughed. "You haven't left much unsaid. I suspect that a lot of Council members have felt pretty much the same way. Part of the trouble has been the structure of the USO, probably inevitable in the emergency. Part has been the inadequacies of some of the employed personnel in dealing with volunteers—they simply haven't known how to give them their best chance to work. On the other hand," he raised a rueful eyebrow at her, "we can't in fairness forget that only you and I are model volunteers! A lot of the others are pretty tough customers and the staff hasn't by any means had a simple job handling its helpers."

"A truer word was never spoken. And if you were listing different groups of people who have given their services without remuneration to the USO, you'd have to put high up on the list the men and women of the staff who have given thousands of hours of extra time beyond any reasonable professional schedule."

"Right. And of course experiences differ in different places. Last month I made rather an extensive tour of our state visiting USO clubs and I found some places where the set-up was exactly as you would want it to be: volunteers who have lived in those communities for years have complete responsibility and the staff confines its activities to administration and guidance."

As they slowed down in front of the club Mrs. Shaw glanced at the clock. "Mr. Davis, I've just barely time to meet the express. A service-woman cousin of mine is coming in. Would you be willing to deliver the cookies for me?"

Mr. Davis was glad to, since it would give him a good excuse for going around to the kitchen door and having a look at things for himself. If what he had heard about the inadequacy of facilities here was true, he would be very much in favor of moving this operation bodily to the large Federal Recreation Building. Mr. Redfield would doubtless be only too pleased to have so competent and resourceful a young woman on his staff of associates. In his own opinion it would be a move in the direction of both economy and efficiency. But he was in the dark as to how the director here would feel about giving up an operation where she had top authority.

It was almost impossible to get near the place through the sea of khaki, blue and white. Evidently the program being carried on here was something the men wanted and enjoyed. Carrying the box of cookies carefully, he went around to the back and immediately saw part of the reason why these quarters were inadequate. In a kitchen so narrow that the six women working at the table, sink, and stove stood almost back to back, sandwiches and salads were being prepared for all the mob out front.

From the back porch he could see there was only one door between the kitchen and the dining room, so that people going out with fresh piles of sandwiches and trays of steaming coffee cups were in the way of people coming in with stacks of dirty dishes.

Another thing that impressed him was the variety of women who went in and out, helping with the refreshments. A few were older women, friends of his wife's; some he recognized as business and professional women from downtown offices and stores. As he stood there a car drove up to the side entrance and five young girls, from their badges and overalls obviously just off the production line at the plant eight miles up the road, hurried in carrying dresses and aprons over their arms. Usually, he knew, the workers at that plant went into the Centerville USO which was two miles on the other side of the plant. Probably these girls had been active in this Agency before the war.

He went in with the cookies and thoroughly enjoyed the fuss that was made over him before he could make himself heard through the general confusion as to their real donor.

He was then informed that Miss Sullivan had been wanting to see him, had in fact planned to drive by his house tonight to consult him about a problem. When a substantial housewife offered to show him where Miss Sullivan was at the moment, he followed willingly. She took him through the two main rooms of the club whose draperies, lamps, and slipcovers impressed him as almost aggressively feminine. Probably that was one thing the boys liked about the place after the bare severity of camp.

"Hello, Mr. Davis," Miss Sullivan greeted him. She was not a bit a managing sort of person and yet when she accosted him like that he always felt pleasantly eager to fall in with her plans. She looked nice, too, he thought, not exactly pretty but neat with rather a flair of some sort. It was pleasant doing business with her, especially since she didn't waste time beating about the bush. This time was no exception.

"Mr. Davis, we've got to do something about this club. If we don't, we're going to lose a lot of our best workers because there's literally not enough space here for them to work in. Don't you think we better move into the federal building?"

So there it was, thought Mr. Davis, as easy as that. "Shall we go over now and have a look at the place, see what quarters might be arranged?"

They went in the club's car leaving two women to whom Miss Sullivan referred as "my standbys," to close up. Inwardly Mr. Davis made a face over her use of the possessive pronoun, as though the whole works were her special property and the volunteer women, her special helpers. Outwardly he let it pass. Maybe he then conceded, when a staff person finished off a day of handling such a collection of people as he had seen in the kitchen, maybe she had some ground for calling the total operation hers. But he mustn't waste this chance to draw out Miss Sullivan's ideas.

"What USO job do you think we do best in this town—from the administrative angle, I mean?"

She considered the matter. "I think it's pretty good the way the Agencies act as channels to bring their own constituent groups into the total USO picture: the Catholics put the women of the sodalities in touch with some of the problems, the Jews open up the way for people from the Jewish Centers to help, the Protestants bring in groups of their churchwomen, men's and boys' clubs, and of course the Travelers Aid have their well-trained workers, lay and professional. I like the way there's just one central place for registering and for training volunteers. Then no matter what their faith, they are interchangeable from one job to another. I wouldn't be surprised if the general interest of volunteers in the advancement of the total program hasn't been partly due to this joint training—their pretty general co-operation, for instance, in making out a weekly club schedule without serious conflicts, letting each club specialize in what it does best: a big dance, or crafts, or home-like atmosphere and small group enterprises."

"I don't hear you including your own specialties."

"You mean work with women and girls?" She laughed. "I guess that's because it seems so obvious to me. But since you ask, there are two things I am concentrating on at the moment. One is trying to make people see that Junior Hostesses must be regarded as individuals in a total community picture—not just as dance partners and nothing else."

"Which is just what a lot of them want to be."

"Exactly. That's why it's going to take a really smart program to keep them balanced individuals under these emergency conditions."

"You would have even more scope for that line of interest in the larger building. What's your other preoccupation?"

"Wives, servicemen's wives. You know they haven't always been awfully cordially received in USO's. But lately," she went on with slightly malicious relish, "with so many men returning home, it has been discovered that wives may be a factor in servicemen's readjustment! So at present wives are enjoying quite an ascendancy."

"You've had wives' clubs and all that since the beginning, haven't you?"

"Oh, yes, and so have a lot of other clubs. Wives are apt to make awfully good workers in a club. They've pretty generally made their way though they weren't very well received at first—either by the men's Agencies or by some groups of Junior Hostesses."

Arriving at the Federal Recreation Building, Miss Sullivan went in search of the building supervisor and Mr. Davis, hat in hand, stopped to watch a fast game of ping-pong. One of the players was laughing as he sent the ball back and back and back. His opponent, a newly discharged veteran, was the more skilled but there was obvious tension in his stroke.

Suddenly, perhaps conscious of Mr. Davis' gaze, he slammed the paddle onto the table and walked straight up to him. Mr. Davis was so startled he stepped back a pace, expecting the man to speak. Instead a moan shook him and Mr. Davis got a glimpse of terror in his eyes before he shut them and leaned on the table for support.

"Get Mr. Redfield," Mr. Davis told a Junior Hostess who was passing. His voice, though low, sent her swiftly after the Director. Meanwhile he got the man a chair. He sat slumped forward, his arms folded on the table, his head down on them.

"The game seemed to be going quite all right, sir," said the man's opponent anxiously.

Mr. Davis nodded as reassuringly as he could, then saw that Mr. Redfield was beside him.

"We'll help him into my office," the Director said briefly.

The veteran seemed to pull himself together as they walked along.

"Would you like me to call a doctor?" Mr. Redfield asked when he had closed his office door, shutting out some of the noise.

"Yeah. Maybe you better. Not a medical doc. One of those guys helps you get hold again."

"A psychiatrist?"

The man nodded. Then smiling shame-facedly, "Guess I saw too much. Can't get loose from it. Know anybody could help me or are they all a bunch of quacks?"

"I'll get you the best man I know. You can talk to him and decide for yourself."

He went outside and made a call, then reported back. "He lives nearby. He'll be over in ten or fifteen minutes."

"Thanks. Could you, sir," he looked up at the Director, "I don't know who you are, but you don't seem to be going any place—" His gaze rested on Mr. Davis' hat. "Could you stick around until the doc gets here?"

"Of course."

"I'll be going along then," said Mr. Davis. Instead, however, he went into the library and in an unoccupied corner took a few minutes to pull himself together. It had been disturbing to see a man collapse like that. He felt new respect for Mr. Redfield who had known so promptly that the USO had no skills for helping any one so seriously disturbed as was this young veteran.

"Oh, there you are!" Mr. Cohen greeted him presently. "I was looking for you. Heard you were back."

"How's our inebriated friend?"

"He wasn't asleep. I've been talking to him ever since you left—two solid hours!"

"What's the matter with him?"

"He's all broken up by his wife's death. Has two little girls and hates to go to war and leave them with his in-laws which, he says, is the only possibility. I just let him talk—seemed about all I could do.

He was sober enough when he left and calmer in his mind, I thought. I did ask him if he'd been to church lately and when he said he hadn't, I made him promise he'd go to mass tomorrow morning."

When the building closed at midnight Mr. Davis came thoughtfully down the steps, paused to fill and light his pipe, then set out at a leisurely pace for home. The breeze, tepid in his face, did not urge him to a brisker gait and his thoughts were as unhurried.

On the whole he believed the USO had done a fair job tonight. It had taken time for these different clubs to acquire the knack of carrying the load among them. It had been no small job to serve thousands of soldiers, sailors, and Marines daily and at the same time work out satisfactory procedures in the course of which the legitimate interests of Catholics, Protestants, and Jews were given due consideration in working plans and in budgeting. That the USO was the vigorous going-concern he believed it was, bespoke much for the fundamental sincerity of the men and women working in it.

There had been some pettiness of course, as there was bound to be in any large enterprise involving people of all sorts. And it had been hard too for some individuals, disciplined in the strict tenets of one faith, to give fair recognition to the legitimate claims of others.

On the other hand, however, there had been many instances where men and women with unswerving loyalty to their own beliefs had found rich working areas in common with people of other creeds. In this fact, Mr. Davis felt, the USO could take real satisfaction. He was glad also to have observed an attitude of respect for military personnel who preferred to remain aloof, keeping their own counsel, not identifying themselves with any creed.

He was aware of many stories, labelled "inter-faith" by some, that told of workers of one creed assisting men of another: the Salvation Army lassie who sent a dejected soldier to early mass; the Catholic and Jewish workers who shouldered each other's work for High Holy Days and Christmas, respectively; the Protestant representatives who helped in the preparation of Jewish ceremonial food; weddings of Protestants arranged in clubs directed by Jewish workers.

These stories had their own significance, no doubt. But to him the far more impressive and heartening thing about USO work was their point of view toward the freedom of religion guaranteed in the Bill of Rights. He had seen for himself in staff and volunteer conferences a concern that the USO do its utmost to insure American servicemen and women the fullest possible opportunity to worship in accordance with their individual beliefs. And in line with this, on more than one occasion, he had observed representatives of one faith or another spur on their colleagues of different credal persuasion to increased diligence for their own people.

This policy had meant that the USO as a whole had helped meet certain needs for religious service by one faith to its own members. Perhaps the most obvious example was the USO's financing of religious kits for men going overseas: one for Protestants, one for Catholics, one for Jews. He recalled too that, through financial assistance by the USO, there had been made available for Catholic servicemen some two million rosaries and for Jewish military personnel such basic materials as prayer books, mezuzahs, and phonographic recordings of Jewish liturgical music.

Thus the three faiths working together in the USO had, in his opinion, given new and fuller meaning to one of the Four Freedoms: not merely that a man might be free to have his own religious convictions but that there might be full opportunity for him to worship as he pleased.

Eight Hour Lay-over

(EXCERPTS FROM A LETTER)

"Dear Dad ... We had a swell trip. The transportation included a Pullman to —— and we had a lay-over of 8 hours there. Dad, I've never been in such a swell USO.

"They had taken the basement of the Opera house and fixed it up swell. The floor space must be a city block square. Immediately inside the front door is an information desk and it is equipped with an amplifier to enable buddies to be paged when they get separated. They have city maps, directories and a couple of girls that will tell you where any place in the city is.

"There are easy chairs all over the place and magazine racks. There is a section of one end reserved for dancing. There is a snack bar where you can buy most anything for a nickel and take it to a table. There are about sixty tables all enclosed by a little railing and every Sunday morning they serve coffee and doughnuts. It was Sunday when we were there and in the center of each table was a big plate of doughnuts and you just walked in and sat down and a hostess would come up and get your order—coffee or milk. All college girls about twenty 1, 2, or 3.

"There was an area of about 30 square feet with newspaper files and easy chairs and a home town paper from every town in the U.S.

Right behind it was a section railed off where you could go in and paint. They had pastels, charcoal, oils and finger-paints and on the walls were all kinds of drawings. Beside it was a booth where you could make a recording of your voice for a dime including mailing. To the left of the art section was believe it or not a section called the cookie corner and on three long tables are endless bread cans each filled with a different kind of cookie. There are tricky signs, paintings and drawings all over the place and the lights are all from lamps giving it a homey atmosphere. They have a sick call where you can go at regular intervals where a registered nurse will patch up blisters, doctor athletes' foot and hand out aspirin. Beside it is a section with about forty or fifty cots where you can go in and take a nap.

"On the other side of the First Aid section is a table where three or four women sew on buttons or your insignia for you. The swellest thing I think is a spot called a pressing parlor. It's a screened off section with about a dozen electric irons where you can go and press your own clothes. In there they have also half a dozen shoe-shine kits and stands where you can get a brother soldier to shine your shoes after you shine his.

"There are also a flock of ping-pong and pool tables and an indoor miniature golf course. A music section where some guy is always playing the piano and fellows standing around singing. Oh Shux I could write all night about some of the things I haven't mentioned but I think the secret of the whole place is the atmosphere. There are no visual leaders. It seems like everyone just sings and so on."

CHAPTER III

Roof Over Their Heads

Mr. Timothy Jones, building inspector for the USO, thoughtfully folded his steel rule and still wearing his hat on the back of his head where he had pushed it when the subject of faucets had been under discussion, got into his car and headed out to the highway. He was through inspecting for the day.

At the crossroads diner he stopped for a cup of strong tea and a piece of pumpkin pie, asking first if it were sweet enough this time, knowing it wouldn't be, no matter what Joe said, but taking it anyway.

He had swallowed only one gulp of the scalding tea when the telephone in the back rang. I'll bet that's for me, he said to himself. It wouldn't be the first time he had been intercepted at this diner. I'll bet I'm not through with this day after all. And even before Joe sang out to him, something inside him was pleased, something made him feel that after all he was quite a fellow—or at least, not a complete liability in the war effort. For somewhere there was an emergency and he was going to rise to it.

"O.K. I'll be there," he said into the telephone instead of "hello." Then almost as an afterthought, "Where is it? What USO is this calling?"

Hanging up the receiver, he told Joe to scramble him a couple of eggs. "Guess I might as well turn this snack into supper. Got to go up

Middleville-way about thirty-five miles. They can't seem to find out what's gone wrong with the heating system. Kitchen keeps smelling of gas." Waiting for his eggs he continued to drink his tea.

There was something curiously precise about Mr. Timothy Jones. Perhaps it was the way he usually set his hat so straight on his rather square bald head. Perhaps it was his socks which were always white or the way he wore his articles of apparel which were scrupulously neat but as ill assorted as though he had got them one by one from a mail order house.

Whatever sense of costuming he lacked was, however, more than compensated for, from the point of view of the USO, by his genius for seeing buildings as the outer shell around warm, inner life—and managing to have them function efficiently in just that way.

A casual observer might have been surprised that Mr. Timothy Jones should have known about such a thing as a warm inner life. But such an observer would not have known about George, his nephew, whom he had brought up from babyhood in an off-hand, tender, practical way that was in itself almost a treatise on parenthood.

Since George had gone overseas, Mr. Timothy Jones had been around a bit in his work. In fact, he had recently crossed the country, stopping off on the way at all sorts of places needing physical housing for USO clubs.

Procuring essential building materials and people to do the work were continuous headaches for all of them these days. Like a magnet the war held industry and manpower centered on itself. Around about and in amongst this war-centered concentration was the everyday life of civilians, of servicemen, and of war workers when off-duty. This every-day and off-duty life was far from normal itself, permeated as it was with emotional strains. Relatively few families were not personally involved. For some, as the war went on, the strain came to a full stop, its place taken by a devastating sense of loss that made living seem no more real than a series of empty gestures.

For more people, however, the strains went on. Sometimes they protectively enlarged peoples' philosophic attitudes. Often they pulled tempers more and more taut and slipped a pervading weariness beneath even the best poised charm. Again they made more simple and more straight-forward the small acts of kindness of everyday people for each other.

Mr. Timothy Jones saw much of this in his travels, picking up the feel of things as he went about his business in the daytime, and as he often sat unobtrusively off to the side at night, sharing vicariously in the heightened life of whatever club he happened to be in when the day was over.

He took note too of the "party-fied ways" that prevailed in most clubs—the niceties, the little jolly thoughtfulnesses, the trimmings that are spontaneous in peace time, but during a war take conscious dedication of a high order to prevent the stern bones of efficiency from showing through.

At other times he took great interest in what he called the "solid front" clubs that he occasionally came across. These were clubs run by people who didn't get along very well together. Sometimes they were of different faiths with little use for each other. Sometimes they were "prima donnas"—male or female—who wouldn't have pulled in harness in any sort of set-up that didn't give them an individual spotlight. But he had noticed—and it warmed his heart—that when it came to the public, the workers in these clubs stood shoulder to shoulder, presenting a solid front of welcome to the servicemen.

On the whole he doubted whether the majority of servicemen knew which Agency ran the clubs they used. All the buildings had only the letters USO outside. Inside there might be a sign stating which Agency was in charge and which were the co-operating Agencies. But he imagined few GIs bothered to look at it. All they knew, or cared to know, was that it was a USO.

Saying goodnight to Joe, he helped himself to a toothpick, conveniently on the counter in a little bowl, slipping it into his vest pocket just in case of emergency. Then he climbed into his car and started down the road. Tonight he rather regretted the thirty-five mile war-time speed limit. Not that there was any danger from the gas escaping into the club kitchen where he was going. It was just enough to be unpleasant and give a couple of the women a slight headache. But when he had work to do, he liked to get there.

Still, he thought as he rode along, if there was any section of USO work that had had to exercise more patience than the building department, he didn't know which it was. He was almost glad he hadn't been working for the USO that first year. The delays then had been something awful, he'd heard. He knew that when the Government signed a contract with the USO in March of 1941, it had agreed to furnish some three hundred buildings. The USO's job was to supply the people to run them, and to make and carry out program plans.

But of course it did take time to erect buildings and even though during most of 1941 we weren't fighting a war, we had our hands full becoming what we were calling then "the arsenal of democracy." Naturally a lot of other things had had to be put ahead of the construction of USO buildings.

The need for club buildings to work in had been terrific, however. More and more men were pouring into the training camps and the Army was urging the USO to get its facilities going to help take care of the soldier's out-of-camp leisure time. Something had to be done. So the Agencies comprising the USO borrowed or rented many of their civilian facilities, and in addition other buildings were pressed into service.

But it wasn't always the easiest thing in the world, Mr. Jones knew, to find a structure big enough and located right for a USO club. Often you had to do a pretty expert selling job about the USO itself before local people were willing to turn over their buildings for USO clubs. And it had been more than a little difficult in the early days to sell an organization that couldn't very well have anything to show for itself until it had a roof over its head so it could get started.

However, the enthusiasm of its backers and the good nature and

good sense of the public had carried the day, and clubs were opened
up in all sorts of places. As time went on these included churches,
a log cabin, a museum, a castle, the barn of a Dutch Reformed Church
manse, beach and yacht clubs, a Quaker meeting house, a former
Buddhist temple, a bank, and fine old mansions at least one of which
had been used for historic background in a Hollywood production.
In such places as these not much adaptation was necessary.

Somewhat more extensive renovation was required to transform
into suitable USO clubs a former newspaper plant, funeral parlors,
dry goods stores, a jail, warehouses, automobile salesrooms, a corner
saloon, gas stations, the training headquarters for nationally known
prizefighters, and a modern greenhouse.

They'd had to use some of the good old Yankee ingenuity too, he
reflected, when the only place for a club in one locality proved to be
two full-sized barracks joined together in an area that literally shook
with the practice guns of tank corps and antiaircraft units and that
had an almost constant cloud of smoke settling in fine soot over
everything.

Two sleeping cars, on the other hand, hadn't required much fixing.
A railroad had turned them over intact to a USO Lounge in a
crowded area to help relieve the shortage of sleeping accommodations.
Each slept forty men and they were equipped with light, heat, bunks,
leather mattresses, pillows, and blankets.

Another structure into the renovation of which he had put special
enthusiasm was a Ku Klux Klan building located out in the woods.
When the USO went in to convert it into a club for Coast Guard
Artillery use they even found the Ku Klux Klan uniforms. A few
months later both Jewish and Catholic workers were holding planning conferences there.

They had sometimes been pushed a little to make cheerful and
homelike quarters out of the morgues and mortuaries that were assigned them. But they had done it as part of the day's work. He remembered too with satisfaction one place where, when the white

owner of a Negro morgue was reluctant to make it available to the USO, some of the leading Negroes in town incorporated a holding company and raised over twelve thousand dollars to purchase the property.

A mule barn had been another tough proposition though the resulting club with its white ramp and fine, broad entrance door had been a prize when finished!

Occasionally, too, a real surprise would come along as had happened when the USO took over an old mansion, claimed by the city for unpaid taxes and occupied at the time by some twenty squatter families. During the renovating, it was discovered that all the beautifully designed fixtures on the first floor were solid silver, goldplated!

Another thing that he enjoyed was fixing up places for the servicewomen. They had several USO clubs of their own across the country, though they were welcome in any USO. In fact some clubs rigged up a special lounge for them with fireplaces, and maybe low coffee tables, and some special modern hangings. And always of course there must be laundry facilities. Washing and pressing were prime requirements of any place aiming to supply what the women wanted.

There was one place where he'd helped plan the redecoration of an old tavern for the servicewomen, and in the long dormitory room where the walls were too queer for anything but plain paint (oyster-white, he'd made it), they had put gorgeous, splashing wallpaper *on the ceiling!* That was the sort of thing the girls liked after all the sameness of their uniforms. And another popular club had an all-mirror powder room, donated to the USO completely equipped with cosmetics.

On the whole the women in the services were easy to please, he thought. They were not much for mass recreation, for doing things all in a crowd. They had enough of that on duty. What they liked was to come into a club in twos or threes and even singly and sit by the fire, read a book, or play good music.

Once Mr. Timothy Jones had attended a party in a servicewomen's

USO. (It had impressed him that there were almost more men there than women—fathers and also boys waiting for dates with the girls.) It had been a party which the Navy had asked the USO to hold for new Wave recruits, their families, and friends. Mr. Jones, sitting erect in a back row seat, had thought this was quite a scheme. It gave the recruiting Commandant a chance to tell about the service. They all saw movies of what a Wave's life was liable to be like. But more important still, he suspected, was the chance this gave each set of parents to look over other parents, and size up the sort of families from which other Waves were coming. It didn't do any harm either for parents to see first-hand the sort of place a USO club was, in case their daughters wrote home that they were using one.

Here he was, at last. Did he just imagine that he smelled gas even while he parked his car? The plumber was waiting placidly for him. He would be, thought Mr. Timothy Jones grimly—the man was too dumb for anybody else to want him, but he was all that could be gotten in these manpower shortage days. Soon it appeared that the plumber could use his hands if directed which he was, immediately and explicitly. Five minutes' work and everything was shipshape. Mr. Timothy Jones, who had privately hoped for an emergency of some dimension because he wanted to counteract his general anxiety about George with a feeling of great usefulness, felt somewhat deflated.

Well, it couldn't be helped. He'd stay a bit now he was here and sing with the boys around the piano. They had some good baritones tonight and a lively lady player. Unbuttoning the top button of his vest and getting ready to expand his lungs, he remembered that this was the piano which had been given to the club because of a picture a GI had had put in the paper. This chap had had a picture taken of his buddy singing with his mouth wide open, and he himself sitting on a kitchen chair going through the motions of playing a piano in the air. Beneath had been the caption, "Yes, We Got No Pianos." Nine had been offered by telephone next morning. In one way or another, he had observed, pianos had a way of turning up in nearly every club. He had even seen one with 1200 autographs carved upon it.

Mr. Timothy Jones sang bass and loved it. While he came in at appropriate moments, his mind wandered among a lot of gifts or loans that USO's had received. All kinds of furniture, of course, plain and period, rugs, lots of fine pictures, and beautiful albums of symphonic music. Free services were just as much gifts too, the way he figured: piano tuning, radio and watch repair, the work on club murals including that of artists from famous studios. He remembered also an outdoor dance and recreation floor that had been built as a gift by two labor unions, four cement companies, and a contractor who gave everything involved. There'd been a pool table once too that some guy had offered to the ladies who were starting a small USO. They fixed a place for it but couldn't figure any way to get it moved until one of them stepped across the street to the firehouse and turned in the alarm for the volunteer firemen. When they came dashing in, full of fire-extinguishing zest, and asked where the fire was, they were told there wasn't any but the USO needed its pool table moved!

Most furnishings and supplies were secured through the USO's central purchasing department. Over a five year period these were to include such items as 27,000,000 paper cups and sundae dishes; three and a half million cakes of soap; nearly a million table tennis balls; over 42 million books of matches; and for letterheads, envelopes, postcards, a grand total of 1,043,150,000.

In cases where central purchasing was not feasible for a given item, the local club might be authorized within its budget to buy the article locally. Every invoice went through the central accounting department of course so that all expenditures were accounted for.

Sound financing for such an organization as the USO had naturally meant that expenditures for furnishings must be kept low. Within the restriction of the budget, however, a definite effort was made to get as much beauty into the clubs as possible. The USO seemed to feel that, in a world where destruction was at the forefront, fine music, good line and color, and even such a detail as a rug under your feet, had stabilizing and reassuring value.

Naturally the USO had credited religion right along, too. In the offices of Agency-conducted clubs were to be seen the Star of David, or a Crucifix, or a picture of Christ. One day he'd seen a Navy Chief who had fought at Guadalcanal and the Coral Sea looking up at the Crucifix in a director's office. Suddenly he had begun talking, to no one in particular: "You don't know what it is out there. Confession sometimes takes quite a while because you have to stop to pick off snipers, but the padre understands. The guns keep firing as you stand at Mass. You have a revolver in one hand and a rosary in the other. . . ."

Mr. Timothy Jones hung on to a final bass note for all he was worth, then gave a half salute to those nearby, and went out to his car. Funny what it did to a man to fill up his lungs and sing—made you feel sort of relaxed and free somehow. No wonder so much singing went on in the USO's. What was the use in varying an activity when it was satisfying in itself? It was natural enough, in his opinion, that there should be much similarity in club programs.

Actually, of course, no two USO's in the country were alike. Each took on differences, inconspicuous or emphatic, depending on climate, the taste and interests of the men and women who worked in them, on the desires of the clientele. Among countless variations some of the more common special features he had noticed included Public Address systems used for all sorts of purposes, including the broadcasting of symphonic records; bowling alleys; bulletin boards, arranged in some clubs by such subjects as cartoons, music, post-war plans, and current news. Maps were frequently on the walls—sometimes Army maps with a daily change in the line of battle represented by a string wound around movable pins. Pressing facilities were frequently available, also shoe-shine equipment. Open fireplaces were appreciated, especially if a basket of oranges was handy or popcorn.

Shelves of books, part of the fruits of the Victory Book Campaign, magazines and newspapers—often from various home towns—were almost standard equipment, as were dictionaries with well-thumbed spots around such words as *buses, maneuvers, fatigue, chevron,* and *believe*. Every club, too, had the USO Bulletin of course so that both servicemen and volunteers could read about what was going on in other parts of the country.

One club he knew about took a picture of every boy who came in. Another had installed a photostat machine to help servicemen or women who had been told to "send a copy" of this or that. A private dining room where small parties could be given for individual servicemen made a great hit in another. Also popular were kitchens in many a club where servicemen were allowed to cook their own food—whether lobsters or spaghetti. Or sometimes an older serviceman and his wife got their own supper there, sat down to it with a tablecloth and silver; then washed up afterward just like old times.

But the endowed doughnut machine took the cake—or the doughnut, amended Mr. Timothy Jones, pleased with his own wit. A thoughtful gentleman had given it to one of the large city clubs, and the boys got such a kick out of making their own doughnuts that the USO had to tell the donor the club couldn't afford to buy so much batter. He was so pleased the GIs were enjoying it that he came through high, wide, and handsome and endowed the thing so the boys could keep right on running it.

While Mr. Jones was chuckling to himself over the endowed doughnut machine, he had turned off the main road and parked beside his favorite USO. Ever since he had received the emergency call at Joe's diner, he had intended to end the evening here but, since he visited the place pretty often when he probably ought to be concentrating on paper work at home, he had not allowed himself to notice his intention until he found he was parked here with the engine turned off. There seemed nothing for it then but to go on in.

He liked this club because they made him feel so terribly welcome—

just as he guessed they did every boy who came through the front door. They were just that kind of people. This time of course they wouldn't pay any attention to him. He opened the door softly so he'd be able to explain to himself that he'd just slipped in, in case nobody greeted him.

"Hello!" boomed a hearty voice before he'd got his head inside. "Where have you been all this time, Mr. Jones? We were saying just the other day that maybe you didn't like us any more. Maybe you didn't want to come to see us except when we needed estimates on repairs!"

Several others came up to shake hands with him and Mr. Timothy Jones was almost overcome. The precision and practicality of his vocabulary gave him no words to deal with the way he felt. Quickly he plunged into his own field and asked how was the new telephone room working out.

Long distance telephoning was made as easy as possible in many clubs. Often the man who had to sweat it out for an hour or more after putting in his call, was made comfortable with a nearby easy chair, magazines, and maybe even a bite to eat. These waiting periods were full of tension, Mr. Jones had noticed, especially for men calling their girls. When such a call finally went through and when the surprised voice at the other end of the line asked where, for goodness sake, the man was, he'd been known to wrench open the booth door and call out, "Where am I?" and upon being told which USO it was, would yell in a great dither, "No, I mean what *state?*"

But the most co-operative telephone volunteer Mr. Jones knew about was the one who was asked by a serviceman one night to play a Hawaiian record on the victrola when he gave her the signal from the booth. Mystified, she did as she was told and was terribly surprised to hear his voice raised above the native music, "I'm in Hawaii, honey. Can't you hear the music? But I'm coming by plane to see you to-night. In fact I'll be there in ten minutes." When he hung up and came over to the USO woman he had added, "And so I will be. She lives just around the corner, but I haven't seen her for eighteen months and I thought this way would give her a big thrill."

They knew at this USO that Mr. Timothy Jones liked to wander around by himself. Tonight as he watched people coming and going he fell to thinking that the bulk of what the USO did was no more spectacular, no more exciting than what goes on in the average American home day after day. This fact was epitomized in the greatly overworked saying that the USO was the servicemen's "home away from home." Bulking large in all clubs—as in most homes—was the cookie jar and the between meal snack. People who worked behind the snack bar said it was a stage changing every fifteen minutes. Boys from every state, boys from all the fighting fronts always hungry, all of them.

How they loved hard-boiled eggs in bowls on the counter! He had seen nine eaten one right after the other by a tall, lanky sailor. There were doughnuts almost always, sandwiches, cakes, sometimes pie, and now and then a special treat like a bowl of potato salad so pretty to look at that mess-hardened personnel could not bring themselves to begin on it until specially invited to. There'd been a headline cake, presented by a local baker, large enough to serve fourteen hundred people. He remembered also another food donation: a bag of grocery-store cookies brought in by a GI—"They're not home-made but I've eaten so many here I wanted to give some too."

Records had been made around these USO snack bars. Four marines chalked one up with a quart of milk and one whole pie each. Or perhaps the laurels went to the soldier who had run out of cash on an emergency furlough, and staved off starvation with four cups of USO coffee and sixteen doughnuts. But certainly pushing them for competitive rating was the sailor, just out of boot camp, who ate three sandwiches with tomato juice and a piece of pie; then left the club; came back, ate three sandwiches, tomato juice and pie; then left the club again; came back once more, and repeated the "snack" for the third time. When the hostess smiled at him, he grinned, confessing he was half starved and thought he wouldn't be noticed if he waited ten minutes between meals.

Sauntering through the crowd toward the game room, Mr. Timothy Jones thought also of the snack bar hostess who told him she had once been led off into a quiet corner by an ungainly soldier who said, please ma'am, could he have a couple of sandwiches in a paper bag, because he'd be all day on the train taking his furlough. He'd never been on a train before getting into the Army, and he was scared to death at the very thought of eating in a dining car with everybody looking at him.

"Hi, mister!" a small boy greeted Mr. Jones as he stopped in the game room door. He recognized the youngster who brought his comics each week to the club.

"Hello, Doug. What you got there?"

"Electric train. Mine. I thought maybe these fellas could help me fix the switches. They don't work just right."

"We got it now, mister," enthused a uniformed cadet, nearly standing on his head in an effort to see what was going on under a tunnel. He straightened into a more normal sitting position, and grinned at Mr. Jones. "This is one swell outfit the kid's got!"

"Let 'er go now, boys!"

"Hey, Jack, easy on the throttle! You'd better stick to flying. It's safer!"

"Looks like the real thing—from 5,000 feet up!"

Then a more mature voice over his shoulder said, "Been wanting to see you, Jones. Oh, not about repairs. Decided to wait 'til spring for those. But about this Servicemen's Advisory Committee we set up. It's working swell."

"Good. Seems sensible that the boys should be asked to make suggestions about what they'd like in their club."

"You bet." Then, "Did you hear about the bunch of women who made all the necessary arrangements to start a USO, though they knew they'd never have very many customers since they were off the beaten path?"

"Just thought they'd do it in style anyway?"

"Sure. So they hung out a USO sign and right off the bat twenty-five boys turned up. The ladies didn't know what under the sun to do with them. So first they made them register and then they just broke down and told the truth. 'Boys,' they said, 'here we've just started this USO and we haven't any idea what you do next. You've all been in USO clubs. What do you do in one?' So of course the boys rose to the occasion and laid out just the kind of a program they wanted, and the ladies saw to it that they had it!"

While they chuckled over this little item, Mr. Jones' friend led him toward the snack bar for a good thick turkey sandwich. "I killed the turkey and my wife roasted it. So, who's more entitled to enjoy it than us? And if I remember rightly you take that coffee black."

While they ate Mr. Timothy Jones was asked what was new in his line.

"Had a fire on the coast the other day. Burned the USO flat to the ground."

"Which branch of the service used it most?"

"The Seabees. In fact they figured it was their club. Seems the USO there had sort of specialized in doing things not only for the Seabees themselves, but for their wives. The place caught fire about three in the morning but word got through somehow to Seabee headquarters. They rushed to the scene in force, helped move the USO to the city auditorium, put their best men on the new wiring and plumbing needed, and had the place in running order quicker than you'd think possible. Then with the full knowledge and approval of their officers a new USO was built entirely with Seabee labor. Sort of warms your heart, don't it?"

His host nodded and in companionable silence they went on with their sandwiches.

Suddenly persistent shouts of "No! No!" from the lounge brought them hastily to their feet and across the hall to the doorway.

It was now the height of the evening and the place was packed. On a portable little platform in the middle of the room a Master of Ceremonies was trying to explain the entertainment about to take place. Every other sentence was interrupted by these shouts of "No!" which Mr. Timothy Jones could see came from a very good-looking young corporal. At first it seemed a joke but soon his shouting got to be a nuisance. "Oh, shut up!" came from several quarters, both hosts and fellow servicemen. "NO!" shouted the boy, louder than ever.

Then the town's leading banker, quite a polished old gentleman, made his way across the floor, took hold of the boy's arm and said, "Hold on, son. What's wrong?"

"Nothing's wrong!" beamed the corporal. "I'm just enjoying myself! This is the first time since I joined the Army I've had a chance to dispute anybody or say, 'No!' It's been swell! Carry on, mister. It's out of my system now. I'm all for whatever comes next."

Kitchen to Use

*The eastern sky was only faintly luminous through the window be-*hind the stove, when Lieutenant Jane Whitmore came into the USO kitchen from the living room davenport where she had slept out what had been left of the night after walking in from her stalled car.

The Director's fatherly assurance that she was more than welcome to the couch—he only wished he had a cot left—had been a big relief. She had dreaded losing a whole night's sleep when she already felt so unsure of herself in the face of this new assignment. He had told her that of course she might get her own breakfast as early as she pleased.

For a moment she stood still in the dim kitchen, not switching on the light, letting the memory of quiet early mornings at home flood over her. How long had it been since she had had an early morning kitchen to herself?

Slowly as she stood there her shoulders relaxed as they had not in many days of this new, unfamiliar life. She walked over to the low stove and putting her palm flat down on the cold, white enamel, thought how she would like to feel the oven warming under it. She had loved to bake things, especially bread. She could remember how good it had smelled as she had slid a loaf off the oven grate and turn-ing it, softly crackling, on its side had slid it out of the tin onto the mixing board. Or it might be popovers she would be making for a Sunday night, glazed to glassiness on their curved bottoms. Or layer cakes, the batter curving away from the side of the pan in buttery folds.

Oh but this was making her hungry. Going softly so as not to awaken other guests, she found the percolator, a glass jar of coffee, and a measuring spoon. While it percolated she would look around for the toaster.

Sitting high on the kitchen stool she used the oven top for a table and ate her breakfast watching the gray sky turn slightly pink, then rush into deep salmon as the rising sun caught the clouds.

The lack of obligation to talk to anyone, the stillness of the kitchen, and the far look to the bright horizon gradually swept clean the straight path to that old self of hers, the one that had known its steady way around. And as she sat there, gazing not so much at the coloring east as at that composed, former self of hers, she became conscious of new power coming to her across that path. Presently it was as if something dislocated were settling comfortably into place. Automatically she drank the coffee, but the toast cooled on her plate, so absorbing, so terribly heartening was this experience of integrating her new life—not with her civilian life—but with the sources of its strength.

Sliding off the stool, she washed her dishes. When she caught herself hanging up the tea towel with a proprietary feeling, she laughed aloud. It sounded genuine even to herself in contrast to the put-on, mirthless thing she'd been hearing lately.

And laughing right-out like that made her feel suddenly keen to get at the day ahead of her. Her superior officer had asked if she thought she could manage this stiff new assignment. Pausing now in the kitchen doorway on her way out and looking back, she nodded soberly but confidently to the tea towel which she always folded in just that way. Manage? She ought to be able to do considerably better than just manage.

CHAPTER IV

Mobile Service

Flexibility was a main characteristic of USO "Mobile Service." When soldiers, sailors, or Marines were unable to go to a club, Mobile Service went to them.

It started that way. When Pearl Harbor pulled men out of large routine training areas and scattered them up and down both coasts of continental United States to innumerable vital assignments in small groups—antiaircraft, key bridges, a tightened shore patrol, and other jobs hushed in military secrecy—when the location of great numbers of men changed overnight from mass concentrations to scattered outpost duty, USO had to make a quick change also.

In that sudden emergency, when furloughs were cancelled and week-end leaves dispensed with, many clubs stood deserted. But it did not take club directors long to begin a substitute service. Filling their cars with whatever they thought the men would like most to have—cigarettes, writing paper, newspapers, magazines, fruit—they drove out into the country, operating under no concerted plan, simply hunting up military personnel now alerted twenty-four hours a day and more grateful for minimum attentions than they had ever been before.

As the first anxious days passed and no more sudden changes came, one man here, another there would say to the itinerant club director,

69

"Could you get us a radio, mister?" Or, "Do you know anybody has an old kerosene stove? It might help us dry this hole out a little." Or, "Here's some dough. Could you get us a few planks and a couple-a pounds of nails? They'll get around to fixin' us with a platform soon but meantime we could rig a kind of raft ourselves to keep us out of the worst of the mud while we man this antiaircraft baby." And every now and then, "Say, mister, do you know any kind lady would wash us a shirt apiece?" Or even, "It's awful to be a brand-new corporal and no thread to sew the trimming on with!" And one by one the directors did these things that first December of the war. The work was quick, haphazard, spotty.

A month later—in January, 1942—organization of a systematic Mobile Service began. But ingenuity and flexibility, instead of being stultified by systematic arrangements, steadily increased as the war went on. They had to. Conditions of transportation, weather, and the nature of the clientele saw to that.

Every conceivable means of getting there was pressed into service as the work developed: cars, horses, weapon carriers, trucks, planes, jeeps, dories, motor life boats, Picket boats, "ducks," LCMs, ice scooters, swamp boats, and sometimes the director's own legs for a few miles when his motorized transportation broke down and he did not want to disappoint the men who were waiting for him and his movie. The Army, the Navy, and the Coast Guard each took a hand now and then towing a Mobile unit whether it was stalled with engine trouble, bogged down in the mud, or lacking traction in some twelve inches of dust.

Hurricanes took out bridges and Mobile directors had to join rescue squads evacuating civilians from danger zones, turn their cars into temporary ambulances, rig up their unit generators to supply emergency power to the military. Snow too—sometimes up to the lettering on the side of the truck—was a threat to an exact time schedule.

Tides as well as hurricanes destroyed bridges and shifting sands could hang a boat on a sandbar even in experienced USO hands. Ice also was now and then a factor to be reckoned with, whether it covered a boat from stem to stern; made a hard glare of the rope ladder a director might have to climb—equipment on back—to board a solitary craft or, floating in chunks, made it necessary for a director in a small boat to clear a channel by using an oar as an ice-breaker. At the opposite weather extreme were radar stations in southern areas where with heavy wooden blinds closed to darken a room for a movie the temperature would swing well over a hundred.

All sorts of places were included in Mobile Service routes. It might be a stockade where at the request of the Commanding Officer training films were shown. It might be a field kitchen where the director dipped his used mess plate with the rest of the engineers, first in a huge container of soapy water, then in a second and a third for final rinses. Coast Guard Fire Boats welcomed him, and men off-duty showed him how a movie screen could be set up in the hold of an old Army scow. Frequently he was summoned into maneuver areas where, with the rest of them, he had to dive into a slit trench three or four times during the showing of a film. He might be on a crash boat when a sudden call would come, and all of his audience would dash off to the rescue of several men, victims of a crash-landing at sea. Again he might find a little group whose quarters were hidden away in a laundry. Or he might be the man referred to in a terse letter written in the summer of 1943 to a father back home by a GI stationed at a Western mountain lookout: "You say you aren't giving to the USO because they aren't doing anything in our town. How do you get that way, sir? They are doing it where it counts. They send a mobile canteen twice a week to this forsaken peak, miles above nowhere, that keeps us from plain going nuts."

This Mobile Service had been no part of the original plan. When USO officers first met in Washington with Government men in February, 1941—ten months before the country went to war—to discuss a proposed budget, it was not known such a service would be needed.

Fortunately the first budget carried a small but sufficient sum for "contingencies" and upon this fund the organization drew that first summer when Commanding Officers in the Pacific Northwest, in Louisiana and Arkansas, in Virginia and the Carolinas, asked for field service for their troops on maneuvers. For the Army, taking advantage of the wide open spaces which this country afforded was initiating a program of field training that was to result in substantial reduction of casualties abroad.

At first these activities were called "war games" but the name was short-lived as the grim nature of this preparatory training became plain. Realistically facing the job ahead the Army made serious business of these maneuvers. Actual battle conditions were simulated to such an extent that the trainee experienced nerve as well as muscle strain. War became real overnight. Men, flat on their stomachs, carrying heavy gear, wormed their way through barbed wire while machine guns, automatically set, fired live ammunition so many inches above their bodies. Death was near at hand and sober consideration was given by many a man to basic values he had never thought much about before. Now and then a trainee coming to the USO trucks for ice water, cigarettes, or post cards would quietly slip a piece of religious literature into his uniform pocket.

Those were the days when the dust was so thick the directors had to keep their windshield wipers running to see through it. Nor was this condition confined to the desert. When half a million troops and 60,000 vehicles moved into any rural area, the dust soon rose in clouds. Showers! Give us showers! rose the GI chorus.

Working in teams, a Government recreation man and a representative of the USO covered as much maneuver territory as they could ahead of time. Since of necessity the Army had selected thinly populated areas, the towns were small—many times smaller than the hordes of men on leave who would swarm into them on week-ends. Merchants were advised to stock up in advance. Community committees were urged to collect all the cots available. Ticking was bought by the bolt to be stuffed with straw for beds on floors—City Hall floors, Lodge floors, any sort of available floor with a roof over it. Most schools were glad to open their showers. Garage hoses were tapped, shower heads installed in all sorts of places. Sometimes a section of sidewalk made the floor for showers, sometimes an open field.

When the load on a town was not too overwhelmingly heavy the local committee was urged to provide as much home hospitality as possible and many a Sunday dinner was dished up to strangers that summer of '41 though often the families who offered them were not too plentifully supplied themselves.

Simple physical comforts were what the men needed those strenuous days—a place to sleep, lavatory facilities, a chance to take a bath, tubs for washing clothes—nothing complicated or mysterious. USO shower baths did, however, help one community solve a mystery that had baffled it. When the Army first moved in there, townspeople had been amazed by a run on nail-polish—all colors—in the five-and-ten and the corner drug store. What, they asked each other in astonishment, could troops want red lacquer for? Presently a small boy, on hand when showers were being taken by grimy trainees, saw brilliant freckles that did not wash off. "What's that on your skin?" he wanted to know. "Fingernail polish, sonny," they shouted back against the roar of hard, sharp spray. "We put it on chigger bites."

One major public relations problem characterized the initial phase of these maneuvers: the hostility of certain civilians to all men in uniform. War had not been declared and the summer of '41 saw much resentment by local citizens of the inroads of these outsiders. To the solution of this problem the USO made a contribution. By enlisting community help for men who so badly needed a touch of home-like comfort, USO workers were often able to make a hostile civilian realize that this was *his* Army and that these men in khaki were just plain American boys with a special job to do.

As the need for Mobile Service increased the work was set up according to Army Corps areas. Maneuver service continued while maneuvers were the order of the day. A feature of the 1943 desert maneuvers service was the Sun and Sand Caravan, which provided USO Junior Hostesses for both Negro and white designations at widely scattered points. Sometimes the camps were able to provide overnight accommodations so that a range of social activities could be included: dancing, sports, swimming, bicycling, picnicking, hiking, or opportunity for leisurely talk with men who had been cut off from any sort of social activity. If cots were available, blankets might be also, but sheets or pillows seldom were. At least one Senior Hostess went with each twenty girls. Where there were no overnight accommodations transportation might be a problem. In one report of the time is the observation: ". . . a sixty mile trip in an Army truck, three or more hours of dancing, and another sixty mile trip in the Army truck to their homes is too much for the girls . . ."

But the boys were grateful. Again and again they loaded the departing Junior Hostesses with the best the PX had to offer in the way of gifts.

At the conclusion of the maneuvers, requests for girls continued to come in from isolated areas lacking recreational facilities and appropriate services were developed under the name of "USO Caravan." Week-end assignments might range from 200 to 800 miles round trip. Sometimes the Hostesses paid whatever direct expense was involved which might be any amount between a dollar and three dollars and a half.

Meanwhile the individual Mobile unit had taken the field. Since the directors of these outfits—professional staff workers, all of them—were in a position to observe matters of military importance, the greatest precautions were taken to insure secrecy. Not only were all USO employees investigated by the FBI but their reports, sent in by number without place identification, omitted all reference to the size of units visited, to the type of work being done by the men they served, to any conditions of military significance. Only toward the close of the war were these restrictions somewhat eased.

Another service performed by Mobile units concerned religious holidays. Christmas plans were carefully made in advance so that all accessible military personnel who wished it were given some sort of opportunity for celebrating. Occasionally a gaily trimmed Christmas tree was mounted on top of the Mobile unit. In the spring Mobile directors often arranged dawn services on Easter. In the spring preceding the Jewish Passover, they carried with them ample supplies of haggadahs (special Passover prayer books) and matzohs (unleavened bread) for distribution to Jewish men in their areas of service.

Quite opposite types of directors were found to be equally successful. One was the director who put himself completely in the background, who so merged with whatever situation he encountered that he was taken for granted—the man with real genius for getting people to do all sorts of things without their realizing they had been led to do them.

Such a director soon had his area alive with group activities: volleyball, horse shoes, pool, basketball, baseball. Often the team of one small post would be urged to challenge another to a championship game. A dinner for the winners would then be given by a community organization whose interest the director had elicited. With a little encouragement school children took responsibility for hundreds of Christmas gifts to nearby posts and for trees and carol singing. Ice or roller skating parties were arranged for groups of Waves or Spars. Beach parties were planned where servicemen and servicewomen entertained each other. Wherever such a director went group activities seemed to flourish of their own accord and a new zest appeared in the off-duty attitude of many service people.

Most Mobile directors had some of this quality. Many also resembled the opposite type of man—the director who was completely and sturdily himself. Instead of merging in the servicemen's environment, he came to them frankly as an outsider, a non-military person who might have been a cheerful civilian relative.

It was a director of this latter sort that a national USO officer set out to visit one late fall. He wanted to see first-hand if, within the limits of its resources, the USO was giving what was wanted. He knew the men called this director "Unc," and he knew a little about his background: that he had retired before the war from a small business which had netted him a comfortable living but had never gripped his enthusiasm. Friends said he had been too wrapped up in people and their problems to put his first attention on making money. When he had heard that a mobile service was to be set up he applied for the job of director in a nearby area. It had not taken his supervisors long to discover that this substantial figure of a man with the comfortable chuckle had natural gifts for such work. They used him first in one part of the country and then another until the program was well under way. Then he asked to be given a more permanent assignment feeling he would do a better job if he were given a chance to become better acquainted with the men he served.

He had had the same "beat," as he called it, for nearly a year when the national officer wrote that he would like to visit him. Unc was pleased at the prospect of seeing "the boss"—impartially he called all officers and supervisors, "the boss"—and he ran over in his mind the different things he would show him. His eagerness to share his job was based on the conviction that he derived more satisfaction from USO work than did anyone else in the organization. "I get to be with the boys," was the way he put it to himself. "The businessmen and social workers who keep the whole works running nationally, who manage the administration and financial end, they're the birds that have the hard job without any of the fun of seeing what it means to GI Joe."

While Unc thought these thoughts, he was carefully painting a railing at one of the more isolated posts. A brass hat was due to pay the place a visit. Everything must be gleaming with new white lead. A seaman, brush in hand, had been hard at it while the movie screen and projector were being set up indoors for the weekly show. Unc had the reel spinning, asked a friend of his in the audience to keep an

eye on it, and then stalked out to the porch where the painting was
in progress.

"How much more you got to paint, son?"

"Clear around to that front pillar."

"Want to see the movie?"

"You're askin' me?"

"Give me that brush. I used to be a painter myself, shouldn't
wonder."

From thinking of the boss' visit, Unc's mind went to the Mobile
unit itself. Hadn't been working any too well lately. Of course this
afternoon when the fan belt broke had been just one of those little
things that can happen any time. One of the Army boys at his last
stop four miles up the road had fixed it for him with the belt out of
his own jalopy. Shouldn't have stripped his own car but the kid
seemed to want to. Another couple hundred miles and the unit would
be due for a thorough going-over. The USO management was strict
about periodic check-ups—said it saved money in the long run to
have the outfits taken care of. He guessed he'd run his into the shop
ahead of time and have her humming when the boss came to visit.

The painting done and the movie shown Unc packed his equipment
and started for the door. This was the moment when he would ordi-
narily begin to look forward to a quiet cigarette as he drove back to
his room in the boarding house. Of course the cigarette shortage
wasn't of any real importance. He knew that. But an end-of-the-day
cigarette on his final lap had become an institution with him and he
missed it. Still, as long as the boys could get a pack a day, there was
nothing to be too concerned about. Civilians would just have to grin
and whistle.

They held the door open for him and helped him stow away the
heavier stuff. He was tired tonight and glad of their young muscle.
Three of them hung around as he slid into the curved-backed driver's
seat. Suddenly from nowhere they produced a package—like a shoe
box only smaller.

"Happy birthday, Unc! Could you use a carton of cigarettes?"

"Could I!" Pleasure boomed in his voice. "But looka here—you fellas need these."

"Sure we do," they agreed cheerfully. "But you're going to keep them. What do you think we've been saving them up for?"

There was a moment of complete silence, then the starter burred. "Well, so long, boys. Thanks." Unc bobbed his head, backed around, and was off. On the first long stretch across the dunes he struck a match, and settling into his seat, inhaled deeply. Then the feeling he had held back for fear the cigarette donors would think him a blubbering old fool, got the upper hand. For a few minutes he found it advisable to cut his speed. "What a bunch of boys!" he muttered.

The logging road over which Unc drove "the boss" some days later, was called a road only by courtesy. It was little more than a cleared space between the trees. The rain was pouring down, driven by a cold wind in sheets across the way ahead of them as they pushed into the back woods.

"Shouldn't wonder if this was a corduroy road once," Unc observed getting his tongue back from between his teeth just in time to prevent its being bitten as they bounced over a series of cross-wise ruts.

"Hope these boys'll have a fire," observed his passenger, tucking an old laprobe closer around the backs of his legs. "I could do with a cup of coffee." Then he grinned around at the comfortable bulk beside him. "Is it out of order to expect Mobile Service to be on the receiving end after such a trip as this?"

Unc laughed. He liked the boss. He didn't pretend he was used to roughing it. He just roughed it anyway. "They'll have coffee all right. I brought them a simply enormous pot the other day. Got it from a Ladies Aid. They'll have it boiling over a fire rigged up under some sort of shelter."

"How long do these 'Wet-Cold' groups have to stay out at a stretch?"

"Two or three weeks. That's long enough to give their different kinds of clothing a good testing out."

"Tents?"

Unc nodded. "And a good old hay barn when they can find it. There's one where we're going now. That's about the only way we could manage to show a movie in such a drip as this."

"I suppose they eat K-rations too and live pretty much as they would under fighting conditions?"

"That's it. Quite a trick to shave outdoors in freezing weather."

"Anybody ever send them any home-made food or would that interfere with the testing conditions?"

Unc looked innocent. "How're you going to keep these good women who live in nearby towns from slipping you a pie or two now and then or a couple of loaves of fresh bread?"

His passenger blandly returned his look. "Should think it might make for bad public relations if you were to refuse them."

Presently Unc put in another word about the area. "They used to do indoor testing out this way too—had what they called a 'climatic laboratory' where they simulated all kinds of weather conditions. I was there one day—on the outside looking in through the windows!—when they had a ninety mile gale rigged up. That would sure let you know whether a fabric was wind-proof or not! Then again the boys would be sitting around in wet clothing with the thermometer at forty below."

"How about pneumonia? Shouldn't think the Army would have to simulate that."

"Funny thing but the boys kept very fit. The medicos watched them mighty close. Their worst gripe was being bored. There was such a lot of waiting around or just doing automatic things with nothing to occupy their minds. For instance they hiked on a moving track to see how far a man could go with a certain amount of equipment at a certain temperature. It was dreary work hour after hour and a little recreation helped."

"But you couldn't go inside those testing rooms."

"No sir!—not at the temperatures they manufactured. But we got them to rig up a little screen on the far wall of the testing room and then we set up our projector outdoors and threw the movie through the window onto their screen."

Ahead of them something was moving along the road. The driving rain and the thin mist rising from the sodden undergrowth cut visibility to such a point that it was hard to distinguish a man in khaki from the road bed.

"Get in, corporal!" called Unc stopping as the car came abreast.

"Thanks a lot, folks. I better walk. It isn't far now and I'm too wet to sit down on your seat." Water was running off his chin in a crooked little trickle.

"Get in!" ordered Unc with such authority that the soldier obeyed. "Live in these parts, son?"

"Up the road about a mile and then down a lane apiece. If you'll just drop me off at the lane, I'll be much obliged, sir."

"Won't think of letting you out short of your destination." But when they were approaching the place where the lane turned off the boss backed the boy up when he objected to Unc's driving him to his front door. "Let's put him out right here as he suggests. The corporal ought to have the stage all to himself for his home-coming."

As they drove on again, Unc thought about this home-coming. He knew the only house on that little lane. He had found it one day when his car broke down and he had had to look for help. The help, presumably the boy's father, had been more jovial than practical and the exterior of the little shack resembled its shiftless owner. Only when he stepped inside had the impression somewhat softened. In the shabby sitting room were a few books and several worn remnants of better living: a tapestry armchair, a tall lamp, a pillared clock. An erect white-haired woman in a drab housedress laid a book down on the corner of an oilcloth-covered table piled with dirty dishes. Getting up with an absent smile of greeting she went silently to see if she could find the wrench her husband wanted. "I'll heat up the coffee if you'll wait," she offered when the tool was finally found in a pile of rusty traps near the woodbox.

He had thanked her but there hadn't been time to wait. As he turned to go he saw a service flag in the side window. Now that he had seen the erect, well-spoken son, he fell to thinking that the war had had some constructive by-products. Here and there boys had a chance for better education and a broader outlook because of their military service.

Aloud he said suddenly, "The USO has bothered over boys nobody paid attention to before. Nobody cared in peace time whether they had any 'morale' or not."

The older man nodded in agreement. "I don't believe we'll ever slip back so far into indifference again. Too many sensible, everyday people have seen for themselves what a decent social welfare program can mean."

They turned a sharp corner and came upon the bivouacers.

"Hi, Unc!" rose the shout almost with one voice. "We thought it was tomorrow you'd be coming. Got a good movie? Got any matches? Where're the sport pages? Sure could use a helmet full of hard candy! Look, Unc, could you mail some letters for us? How about a couple of new packs of playing cards—we can't get ours dried out."

"Hello, fellows," said Unc unhurriedly, shutting off the motor and preparing to get out. "Have you got any extra rain equipment handy for the boss here? He's visiting us from national headquarters."

"How'd a blanket do? We don't have any spare outfits this trip."

"A blanket would be fine, Mike. Hello, Teddy, how's your wife? That's good. I knew she'd be all right with that bang-up good doctor you made her go to."

"Say, Unc, I gotta talk to you a minute while the movie's running."

"Okay, Herb. Come around. Now how about some good hot juice of the coffee berry. Us oldsters are all stove up with the wet and cold."

"Where next?" asked the visitor a couple of hours later as they headed out of the woods. The rain had stopped and the sky was slowly clearing.

"Hospital."

They rode in silence for a mile or two, then Unc relaxed into a comfortable slump behind the wheel. "Like to tell you about a chap who worried the life out of a few of us for awhile," he said. "There's a little island where we serve a small installation. Terribly rocky place to get to. We come as close in with a boat as we can. Then we have to unload into a sort of big bucket contraption and they swing us ashore in a hoist. Anyhow there's a soldier there who's been out of the country for three years, not in combat but they call him 'Overseas Oscar' just to get his goat. He was the butt of all the jokes, partly because he took it so hard, partly because he hollered back with such abusive language. It didn't take the men long to discover he was terribly jealous of his wife who lived not far away on the mainland. None of them had ever met her but whenever this fellow was stuck on the island and another man had a pass, they would give him a dig and say that so and so was probably out with his wife. It went so far that he began to believe the stories they made up about her and to resent the ragging of the men. Things were going from bad to worse with him getting caught in a vicious circle. He got to be insubordinate and unco-operative in Army affairs. Then he lost his passes and was stuck with KP. He thought the top sergeant was out to get him but actually the topkick wanted to give him a hand."

"Do you ever get called in on these cases?" the visitor asked.

"I did on this one—after awhile. I'd like to get your reaction to what—"

"Hey there, Unc!" came a lusty yell from a dried-up brook paralleling the road, "Give a fellow a lift, will you?"

Unc promptly came to a stop and leaned forward past his passenger to see who had hailed him. He thought he recognized the voice but what could the corporal—and an MP, too—be doing away out here a good five miles from camp? Taking his time the corporal came up the steep bank, both hands full of pebbles. He was a broad, stocky man with clear gray eyes set rather far apart.

"What you got?"

"Might be something pretty good—native jade, I guess they call it." He got in, nodding absently to the other passenger, and poured his pebbles on a little clear space of truck floor, pushing them around with a blunt, dusty finger. "Look at this one now! File and polish her carefully and she'll be a honey." He went on poking. "Hope I can find another one to match—then I can make a pair of earrings."

Unc chuckled to himself. He could see his visitor thought earrings were queer trinkets for such a man. But the MP was explaining. "Unc here got us a swell set of jeweler's tools, sir, and some lucite scrap. We've made quite a pile of nice stuff for our wives—actual or to come." Then looking steadily at the stranger he added, "Seems like a fellow's just lost in the Army if he hasn't got a hobby to take up the slack."

A large hospital area appeared on the left and Unc slowed up. "We're due here to show a movie, corporal. Hope you can get a ride the rest of the way."

Carefully the amateur jeweler picked up the stones and stowed them in his pockets. "Thanks for the lift." He stood erect and gave them a brisk salute, then remembered something. "Say, next time you hit our place, Unc, bring along some of those old toothbrush handles the school kids collected for you. Some of the fellows want to try their hand at those fancy signet rings you showed us."

"Sure will. So long."

They slowed for identification at the hospital gates, then turned into the long curving drive.

"You were telling me about the overseas husband who was getting a little out of hand," the passenger prompted his host.

"Oh yes. Well, one day I was a mighty embarrassed spectator of a pretty serious offense. The man absolutely refused to execute an order given him by the topkick in the presence of an officer. I felt awful about it because I knew the fellow was all stove up inside and that the gang had got him in a pretty bad way. When the kid had gone, the sergeant confessed to the officer that he was at his wits end to know what to do with him. They talked it over back and forth in an understanding sort of way, both of them recognizing that the situation wasn't altogether the kid's fault. Then suddenly they turned to me and asked what would I advise. I said why not give him a chance to excel at something so that he could get his self-respect back."

"Not a bad idea," agreed Unc's companion. "How did it strike them?"

"They asked how it could be done. So I said I'd teach him to operate a motion picture projector. Then the officer could issue an order that this man was officially appointed motion picture projectionist for the Army machine on the island, that he was authorized to service it, and that no unauthorized persons were to do the operating."

"How'd it work out?"

"He was quick to learn. When he seemed to have mastered the technique I let him run the USO movie a couple of times under supervision. Of course at first if there was the slightest hitch, they rode him unmercifully. But he was too occupied getting the thing to work to let out much of a blast at them in return. Then as he got more and more expert with the machine, he became so sure of himself his retorts grew so mild it was no fun picking on him any more."

"Nice work," approved the visitor.

"Yeah. That kid was just plain lucky, having a fatherly sort of topkick."

Unobserved the boss gave Unc a quizzical look.

The ward of the hospital where they were to show the movie was divided into four sections by partitions. This meant that all the beds had to be pushed to the center so that everyone could see the screen.

In the far corner of the last partitioned section with his back to the screen was a Negro boy who could not be moved.

"Don't bother about me," he insisted gruffly. "Just go ahead."

Unc gave him a friendly wink and went off to find his guest who was talking to a couple of fracture cases. "We've got to get that boy away over there in on this party. Now how are we going to do it?"

The boss turned around and had a look at the situation. "If we had a full-length mirror—"

"Why sure! You've hit it. Of course we can get a mirror, prop her up in the window by the kid's bed and reflect the picture to him! Swell idea—you're earning your passage, boss!"

"Then turn the sound up loud enough so he can hear—"

Everything worked out perfectly until the picture was half shown. Then the sound track went bad. Unc stood up and tightened his belt. He spoke into the dark. "Well, fellows, I guess you'll have to put up with me as interlocutor from now on."

It was rather a silly, romantic picture which made it easier to burlesque. Unc had already seen it more than a dozen times so he found it no trick to fit words to the action. He soon had the audience howling with delight at his dialogue and asides. It was a cinch, he knew, to make the sappy story ridiculous—anybody could have done it. Still he was no end pleased when the boss congratulated him. He used the word "wit," but Unc knew well enough it was just his ornery sense of fun.

It was nearly midnight when they drove into the town where they both were staying. After leaving the hospital they had stopped at a Prisoner of War camp. The wind was blowing a gale down the wide slopes where the guards had to pace all night. They had a tough assignment, Unc knew—these guards. The native populace sometimes took out on them their resentment of the German prisoners. He had collected a number of second-hand thermos bottles in his travels and had handed them out to a bunch of the guards so they could have something hot to drink in the middle of the night to help warm them up.

"Do you want to go back to the hotel now?" Unc asked as they waited for a light to turn green. "I've one more stop but maybe you're fed up."

His passenger protested against being left out of anything and asked what the next stop was.

"I like to be around handy Saturday nights when the boys come out from midnight Mass. There's no very good place open where they can get a bite to eat that time of night. I usually get in from my rounds in time to go by the house, make up some fresh coffee, and load in a bunch of cookies. The ladies of the town are mighty fine about keeping me supplied."

They parked across from the cathedral and switched off the motor. Through the cold stillness from several blocks away came the unhurried toll of the town clock, the bell-tone a little flat. The two men glanced up at the unpretentious spires of the cathedral silhouetted against a blue-black sky where scudding white clouds caught the moonlight. The clang of the bell vibrated over the roofs of the little town where most of the lights were out.

There was a moment of clear, cold silence. Then feet were noisy on the short flight of steps—the quick tread of heavy Army boots as men came from Mass singly, or in twos and threes.

The two older men watched as the soldiers discovered the Mobile truck and headed in their direction. Here and there other men in uniform, sauntering the deserted streets, came along too.

"Makes you worry less about the world somehow," one of the men in the waiting truck said quietly, "knowing some of the boys go to services. I happen to be a Protestant myself. But in the last analysis it's all the same God."

His companion nodded. "And for my people too—under the Star of David."

"Hi, Unc!" Off came a sailor's hat above a broad grin.

"Swell to see the USO coffee wagon here again tonight!"

"Good evening, mister," to Unc's passenger. "Pretty damn chilly, ain't it!"

We Thought You'd Like to Know

It was mid-morning when Lester Fulton came along the red slate flagging to the back of the house and clumped up the shallow steps to the sunny stoop. With his hand on the latch of the kitchen door, he paused and looked back over his shoulder. He liked the view: meadow and pasture and thinning woods. He and his son, Henry, used to sit there on summer evenings when the chores were done, chairs tilted back, not saying much. He had missed those evenings this past summer with Henry off to the Army.

Snapping down the kitchen latch, he carried in his half bushel basket for his wife, Maria, to see. "Not more'n a couple dozen apples on Henry's tree this fall. Looks like it ought to have a bumper crop next year—for his long furlough, maybe. Nothing like Northern Spies, he always said, for making pies. Remember how he liked apple pies, ma?"

She didn't answer but he hadn't expected her to. He was more apt to talk about Henry out loud than she was.

"Henry's not the only fellow likes apple pies!" He meant it to sound jocular but he knew it didn't.

"What'd you think I got my hands in now if not pie crust?" said Maria. "I saw you going up the lane toward the orchard." But inside her mind she was remembering how Henry had said, "I'm no letter writer, ma. But don't you worry, I'll be all right." It had been weeks, though, and no word of any kind.

The hardest thing, she thought, crumbling the little balls of flour

and lard, was the awful uninterrupted way everything else went on—
as though the meaning hadn't dropped clean out of life. The days
and weeks dead-level and, underneath, the fear you couldn't argue
down that something had happened to him, that the silence was due
to more than his not being much of a writer.

"Sounds like the mailman's car," said Lester all at once. "He's ahead
of himself today." Maria went with him, her hands not wiped quite
dry she hurried so washing off the pie crust dough.

The mailman always shouted back some remark as he drove on,
"You got a card from the USO folks on the coast."

"The USO?" asked Maria sharply as they turned back toward the
house. There was the card on top of the *Gazette*.

"Yeah. It's to both of us: Mr. and Mrs. Lester Fulton."

"Lester, is he all right?" she cried in a rush of worry. She leaned
across his arm as he turned the card. *We thought you'd like to know
that your son, Henry, was in our club today. He looked fine and when
I asked him for his home address so I could send you this card, he
said, 'Say hello to them for me and tell them if anything goes wrong,
I'll sure get them a letter written.' I saw him drink three bottles of
milk while he was here and he said he'd just finished off a whole
apple pie, so you needn't worry about his appetite ...*

"That's him!" cried Lester. Their hands touched. They just stood
there under the high silver maple that arched the walk, the leaf patterns moving gently over their faces, schooled to immobility. Maria
held her chin steady while through her body went such waves of
relief as seemed would never end. Then Lester laughed, a great burst-
ing laugh. "A whole apple pie, ma! That's him, all right. That's
Henry."

CHAPTER V

The Community at Home

Mrs. Morris did a household errand, then decided to walk to the USO instead of trying for a bus. It was only nine-thirty in the morning but she had dressed carefully in her beige gabardine suit, now in its third year, which would be appropriate all through the fourteen-hour day ahead of her. On her head was a little affair of velvet and flowers that she would take off or wear depending on the formality of her duties. Over her arm she carried an old camel's hair coat, both because autumn evenings were cool now and because she might need it for a cover-all if manual labor had to be performed, as was often the case in these days of meager janitor service.

Walking briskly along, she did not dwell on this matter of janitor service. But she knew, as did many other women working at the USO, that there were times when a hard physical job in a semi-public place where you simply could not break down, was the only thing that kept you going. It had been that way with her when her lovely daughter Harriet, a Navy nurse, had had to parachute from a defective plane and, landing in an apple tree, had injured her spine. It had been weeks before they were sure she would recover. And her son, Bob, was a Lieutenant (jg) in the South Pacific so she knew what it meant to live under strain that never left you for a moment.

As she neared the club she wondered what special problems the day would bring. This was the night for their weekly dance but they were accustomed to its responsibilities. Compared to those early hectic days, dance nights now ran on systematic lines without, she hoped, loss of zest and spontaneity. It was wonderful the way the men and women in the community, and the young girls too, had taken hold, signing up for regular assignments. With one general office worker, named Peggy Ryan, they managed fairly well.

Of course, she thought with pride in her town, they could do it only because there was so much trained skill at their disposal. Business girls helped with the books, young married women who had had office or executive training took over definite sections of the work. And the indefatigable Junior Hostesses danced and took part in all sorts of miscellaneous activities so that their guests from the services would have a good time at the club. She could understand why all the young things rushed into hostessing at first—the attractive ones because of the glamor of the military, the unattractive ones because anything in uniform was a welcome change from sitting at home unwanted. Their USO owed a lot to the woman in charge of Junior Hostesses, Mrs. Laughton, who had seen from the first that these young girls, no matter what their motives, needed realistic training about their attitudes and behavior at club functions. From National USO headquarters they had secured useful material on essentials, for all sections of the country were discovering the same need for training. And after a rather stiff sifting process which Mrs. Laughton rigidly adhered to— and so won the complete confidence of the mothers of the town—the Junior Hostesses were by and large a skillful lot.

The wonder to her was how they could keep at their job, as time went on, with such fresh enthusiasm. There was nothing automatic about their cordiality or their interest in their guests and yet long ago the glamor must have worn thin. For some this training had meant a social poise that they would keep. For others it had meant a new focus that at least temporarily removed their own little selves from the center of the spotlight in favor of a more impersonal friendliness.

Mrs. Morris turned into the flagged path leading up to the neat white frame building that had once been a rather special private school. Mrs. Conrad would be at the desk this morning. She must ask her how she had made out with the lanky sailor she had taken home after last week's dance. He had come in for a sack just as the dance was ending, unaware that on dance nights their few beds were all spoken for by nine o'clock. He looked so downcast at not securing one that Mrs. Conrad had offered her studio couch.

"How'd I make out?" Mrs. Conrad laughed when questioned about the evening. "Do you know we sat up until all hours eating cake and talking and finally he asked would I mind reading his accumulation of mail. You know," ruefully, "I think that was the best night's sleep I ever didn't have! Now about this training course for new volunteers we've been working on—wish you would come to the committee meeting this morning."

"I'd love to."

Mrs. Conrad expressed her appreciation and went back to the agenda she was revising, while Mrs. Morris remarked to herself, as she often had before, how lucky the USO was to have this woman's help. Through her influence the most capable Catholics in the town had become a perfect bulwark of service. And it wasn't just the club that was lucky, either, or the men whom these women served. It was all of them who had a chance to work together. She thought too of Mr. and Mrs. Goldstein and their group of Jewish acquaintances—firm friends of the USO and hard workers in it. She would never forget an incident of the hard weeks when the Goldsteins' boy, Philip, was reported missing. Mrs. Goldstein had told her that the Methodist minister, with whom she had served on a USO committee, had telephoned her at the first report to offer his sympathy and the same afternoon Mrs. Conrad had asked if she might light a candle in her church for Philip's welfare. Somehow Mrs. Morris felt that when things like that happened among people in a town who had never had a chance to know each other before, the town could never settle back into its old narrow grooves.

"Any mail of special interest?" she inquired of their one office employee, Peggy Ryan.

"Just a note from a guy in Australia who'd like us to send him six sets of Staff Sergeant chevrons. I'll try to round them up during my noon hour. Oh, and here's a report from National headquarters about some of the things clubs like ours are doing. It comes from the Division of Community-Conducted Operations. That's us, isn't it?"

"That's us. The other kind of USO club is run by one or more of the National USO Agencies."

"How come? I mean why don't they run us? I've always been meaning to get to the bottom of that."

Mrs. Morris laughed at the girl's funny expression of bewilderment and explained that in the early days the need for the USO-type of service had sprung up all over the country wherever there were large concentrations of servicemen on leave. "No new national organization could possibly expand fast enough to take care of all the places. So many communities had to handle the job as best they could themselves—just as we did here. Then later on we became a USO like most other places."

"But we raise a lot more money in the national campaigns than we ever get back from the national USO."

"Of course. Every community raises its share of the money needed to run the entire USO. Then adequate funds are allotted so that every local USO can do its job whether the amount is more or less than that particular place raised in the campaign."

"Say it again," begged Peggy.

"All right. It's the American people as a whole who want this job done, isn't it? And all the servicemen and women ought to have a chance at it no matter where they happen to be stationed, right? That means that more work has to be done in some places than in others and so the money, collected from all over the country, is divided up on that basis. If a new training camp should be located near us here, we would need much more money than we are getting now, and if the rather small camp we do have should close, we probably wouldn't need any more money at all."

"Oh," said Peggy. "I didn't know it was that simple."

"The best story in this batch," she announced presently, "is the one about a bunch of Wacs at a USO somewhere down in Louisiana, who were given a chance to go out and pick cotton. Afterward somebody asked the old Negro who drove them out what kind of pickers he thought they made. His verdict was, 'They sure was slow but awful clean.'"

It wasn't quite time for the committee working on the volunteer training course to meet so Mrs. Morris decided to take a quick look around the club as she usually did on her days in. As she started away from Peggy Ryan's desk she noticed an erect young sergeant standing by himself at one of the lounge windows looking out. She turned to Peggy and raised a questioning eyebrow.

"I don't know anything about him. He came in soon after I unlocked the door, got three cups of black coffee at the snack bar and two packages of cigarettes. I thought he seemed restless. Twice I started across the hall to ask if I could be of any use and each time I felt he didn't want to talk because he quickly busied himself with something."

"Better just leave him to himself. There aren't too many places these days, Peggy, where a man can think his own thoughts undisturbed." She glanced at him again before she went downstairs and wondered if the erect shoulders weren't second nature to him rather than an indication of an attitude toward life. At least the angle of his head seemed to her despondent.

In the renovated laundry several volunteers were sorting and bundling magazines to be used on ships. Mrs. Morris had scarcely begun to help when Peggy's voice rang down the stairs. "Oh, Mrs. Morris, you're wanted on the 'phone."

It was a neighbor of hers in the country asking if the USC could use his apple crop. "We've picked all we want ourselves. There're just the two of us now with the boys away and we thought some of your gang down there might like to come out and pick them. I've plenty of bushel baskets if you could bring the USO station-wagon and yours too, if you don't mind, to haul them in. Our one truck has only three tires at the moment."

Everybody was delighted. Here was a casual refreshment problem solved for weeks to come and an afternoon's entertainment provided also—more than one, in fact. They'd make a preliminary trip today and size the situation up. Then, if the donor's good nature held, they could organize a hike for Sunday afternoon when they had their largest crowd and let it end at the orchard.

Around noon as the committee meeting was breaking up, a bus from the camp deposited about a dozen soldiers at the club door, one Wave, and a couple of Wacs. The Wacs went on up the street but the Wave made such a bee-line for the club that Mrs. Morris wondered if she had anything special on her mind. "Hello," she smiled, feeling the least she could do was make her welcome, then noticing she was one of the prettiest youngsters she had seen in uniform. Something like quick understanding flashed between them—reward for herself, Mrs. Morris felt, because of having a daughter of her own.

"What would *you* do," asked the Wave, and the despair in her voice was no less real because she smiled, "if you'd just met the man-of-your-life, were going to have a date with him this very afternoon, knew just the kind of dress he would like—NOT Navy blue!—and then, gosh durn it, all you could do would be to put on a clean blouse!"

Mrs. Morris laughed. How good it was that being in the services was not altering these youngsters! She looked at her watch. "In about an hour and a half two station wagons are heading for an orchard where there are bushels and bushels of apples to be picked. I think we could squeeze another couple in."

"AND—," the Wave was almost whispering with the excitement of what was being made clear to her, "for active sports *the uniform is not required!* Picking apples *would* be an active sport, wouldn't it? I'm a good tree climber."

Suddenly Mrs. Morris had the breath squeezed out of her and a kiss on her cheek. "There's a sport shop two blocks up the street on the right-hand side," she answered the girl's next question before it was asked.

The Wave went off on the double quick and Mrs. Morris did what she had been meaning to do all day: walked straight up to the erect young sergeant who was now in the library holding a book, and said, "The USO has just been given a lot of apples but they're still on the trees. Some of us are going out this afternoon to help pick. We'll bring back what we can in bushel baskets. I'll be driving one station-wagon. Could I get you to drive the other?"

"Just people from the club? No officers?"

"No officers so far as I know. Come on. We really need your help."

"I'd like to very much. Should we take a ladder along perhaps and some pails to pick into?"

She agreed, told him where he could find both, and wondered as he went for them, why he had asked about officers.

By two-thirty the two station-wagons were bulging with apple-pickers, both service personnel and Junior Hostesses. Mrs. Morris, behind the wheel, turned far around to see how many had climbed into hers when a familiar voice through the side window said, "I'll drive, mother. May I take Peter?"

"Harriet! I didn't know you were anywhere near here!"

They made no attempt to cover up the moment's pause when neither could speak. These were days when feelings had to be taken as they came along.

"But who's Peter?" demanded Mrs. Morris.

"There he is. Peter, this is the better of the two Morris women."

"Of all the backhanded remarks," said Mrs. Morris, shaking hands with a very ugly member of the fighting forces and liking him at once. "And now I suppose I have to squeeze you two into this conveyance."

"Don't give me a thought," said Harriet. "I'm going to drive. Haven't had my hand on a car for months. You and Peter just manage the best you can."

Afterwards when she looked back to that sunny, windy afternoon in the apple orchard several things stood out, all of them against the ever-present realization that Harriet was home again—probably for only a short leave since she hadn't let them know, but home where her mother could catch a glimpse of her, hear her laugh, protest her lively high-handedness, shake her head in amazement at the number and variety of young men who were always turning up.

Nagging at her own personal happiness had been also concern about the sergeant who drove the other car. He was not in the least handsome but he looked intelligent, and she had felt even in the brief words which had passed between them that he had had more advantages of up-bringing and of education than their GIs often had. When their host joined them toward the close of the afternoon, she spoke to him about the boy and she saw that presently he spoke to him.

"Doesn't seem to be anything special the matter with him," he reported. "A little absent-minded, perhaps. I asked him how long a leave he had and when he woke up from whatever was preoccupying him, he said it was up at twelve tonight—not our camp, the artillery crowd down at the Fort. So I said, 'That's fine. You won't have to pull out till the ten o'clock bus. That'll give you time for the first part of the USO party anyway.' Then I told him that judging by what my wife said, it was going to be quite a dance and we'd be mighty glad to have him there for as long as he could stay."

Looking across the basket of apples to the young sergeant Mrs. Morris did not feel, however, that he looked like a man much cheered by the prospect of any sort of festivity.

All at once the day seemed wearing and Mrs. Morris walked up to the house to see if washing her face and redoing her hair would help. In the bedroom where the women and girls of the party had been asked to leave their things she found a Wac—probably one of the pair who had come on the bus with the pretty Wave. The girl was sitting alone in the half-dark, evidently none too anxious to be disturbed. When Mrs. Morris turned on the low light by the dressing table and began to do her hair, the Wac suddenly burst out, "Look at me! Just look at me! I'm all wrong!"

There was such a wail in her voice that Mrs. Morris went over to her, comb in hand. "What do you mean, child? What's the matter?"

"I'm all fixed up for 'active sports'—first time out of my uniform for twenty-four months. I went to the best sport shop but I look awful!"

She did indeed. Mrs. Morris was spared comment, however, for the girl plunged into an account of herself. It was not too unusual a tale though Mrs. Morris listened sympathetically. Brought up in a small town by a severe aunt, she had become a stenographer and had taken a job in a large city office. She had received a good salary and had spent most of it on clothes. They were, however, always the wrong ones. "They didn't somehow go together—just like these don't. I never looked like the other girls. And what's more I didn't have a thing in common with their glamor-girl, rich-old-wolf talk. The minute I got into uniform, though, everything changed completely for me. I made more friends in a few months—good friends—than I'd ever had before. I didn't have to think—once—about what I had on my back. I could just give the job everything I had."

"So what's worrying you?"

"I'd forgotten what it was like to wear the wrong clothes—like these. I'd even forgotten that I'd have to go back to that shut-in job at the office. When I put these 'active sports' clothes on and saw how wrong they are for me, I realized suddenly what I'd have to face when I'm discharged."

Mrs. Morris asked what kind of work she had been doing in the Army, found she was attached to the Special Services office and was helping with dramatics—"Scene painting, all that sort of thing."

"Then why not go on with that when you get out?" And Mrs. Morris, mentioning several contacts that might be useful to her, was pleased to see her discouragement change into interest. Perhaps an occupation she liked wouldn't automatically improve her taste in clothes, but at least they wouldn't be the matter of prime importance to the people with whom she would work.

A number of different people served as hosts and hostesses at the party that night. There was no doubt the town considered this its club and meant it to be a pleasant, useful place for servicemen and women. Ways of offering hospitality were necessarily as varied as were the wishes of the young people crowding the building to capacity.

Across the country similar clubs were having much the same experiences, Mrs. Morris was aware. There might be snow and firs outside the windows or sand and palms with every shade of variety between. But inside the clubs general activities and individual experiences could not differ greatly since the ways of dealing with both homesickness and exuberance were limited and must be much alike wherever Americans were hosts and other Americans were guests.

Orchestras, easily heard some distance from almost any USO's front door, pulled hurrying Army boots into their insistent rhythm and exaggerated the energetic rolling gait of sailors and Marines. Inside USO's, Junior Hostesses, as energetic as their partners, spent the evening doing square dances or something much more modern. Nor did dancing have a monopoly of activity and noise. Typewriters pounded ceaselessly writing letters home. Across ping-pong tables whammed shots as quick as the jeers and cries of the players and the tap of balls on the pool tables was hardly audible above the fast roll of the bowling alleys. At the piano, three or four enthusiasts, leaning close to follow the music on the rack, might be shouting the words of a new song and keeping time with their feet. Only when the orchestra stopped playing could the faithful jukebox be heard and perhaps a victrola in some far corner where a classical-minded boy was listening to a symphony.

Milling constantly through USO rooms across the country were servicemen with Junior Hostesses or older men and women, talking, laughing, hailing one another. And through the outside doors men came and went all evening checking sea bags, suitcases, coats, occasionally some strange article from the South Seas or a pet—puppy, kitten, bird, turtle, and once or twice a snake; now and then a baby too, when he and the little woman wanted a peaceful supper somewhere by themselves.

Senior Hostesses, never quite hardened to the perpetual uproar of one of these mass entertainment evenings, were amazed in one club to see a sailor settle himself comfortably and unconcernedly in a lounge chair in the center of the din, tip his hat over his eyes and go peacefully to sleep. Over his head blazed a hundred watt bulb and men and girls shouted to each other across his inert form. Finally one n.otherly soul roused him enough to tell him there was a nap room on the floor above on the quieter side of the building.

"Don't bother me, lady, *please!* This is the first good rest I've had. Took a room in the best hotel last night and didn't get a wink of sleep because the quiet was so awful! Here's another nickel for the jukebox. Let her blare away so I can relax."

Intermissions were short because for the man on a pass the whole evening was not long. In the club where Mrs. Morris worked a special dance gave the evening a fresh turn. From a basket tied with red each GI drew a slip of paper and the girls did the same from one trimmed with blue. On each man's slip was the first line of a well-known song. *Dance with the girl who has your second line—*

Over in a corner where his eardrums were not so deafeningly assailed the town's testy old judge, square-faced and white haired, found a boy from Wyoming who was worrying about the taxes on a ranch he had just inherited from an uncle. Ungraciously but with reassuring authority the judge took over, said he'd get a former colleague of his, living somewhere out there, to advise him in the matter.

"Write down your name and where I can get hold of you," he ordered. Then with as much persistent fierceness as though he were cross-examining an opposing witness, he asked innumerable details about the property and so overwhelmed the boy with legal verbiage and a sense of competence—which the judge undoubtedly possessed— that the young ranch owner, leaving the terrible old man behind him at the club, felt he had left also the terrible burden of his worry.

And now the trumpeteer was on his feet, a clear, hard shaft of sound against the muted orchestra—

But even he was ignored in two little rooms at opposite ends of the attic. In one, three men sprawled in worn, over-stuffed chairs, the air blue with smoke from their pipes, but it was Beethoven's Fifth they were there for.

In the other a young father was alone with a borrowed projector and on the white plaster wall again and again ran a movie of his one-year-old son whom he had not seen.

Downstairs again a solid and hearty Marine was singing a song while the orchestra idled. Mrs. Morris heard three girls in succession ask the silent young sergeant to dance. She couldn't hear his reply but each went away smiling while he continued to brood.

Then the black-out siren wailed and in sixty seconds everything was dark. Peggy Ryan made for the piano and now in the sudden hush that pushed at your ears came the somehow comforting melancholy of "Old Black Joe." Everybody sang, safe in the anonymity of darkness, and dozens were a little sorry when the lights blazed on again.

Couples who had plumped down at card tables when the siren sounded, lingered for checkers, double-canfield, or cribbage. Then food was brought in—apple pie with freezer ice cream. Up on the bulletin board while they ate went the evening's best finger-painting. "At least," someone remarked, "you don't feel tied down by the subject."

A Paul-Jones was called. *Right, left, dance with the ninth young lady*—

The community hospital telephoned. Pop White needed some blood. Was there anybody at the USO who could give some? Pop, now over seventy and a veteran of the Spanish-American War, had at one time served more hours in the club than any other worker. Of course they'd get somebody there in a hurry. It took only the telling to those nearest the 'phone—everybody knew Pop. "We'll all go," shouted a bunch and dashed out the door.

The center of the dance floor had been temporarily cleared for the performance of two tap-dancing sailors who were volunteering their act. Mrs. Morris noticed that a nice looking student pilot was standing next to her as all of them on the sidelines kept up a rhythmic clapping for the amazing pair. She had noticed this young trainee before during the evening for something about him reminded her of her son— nothing more than the deep sunburn, perhaps, and the crisply waving hair, once probably a darker brown, now bleached to the same glowing tan.

Through the persistent noise he spoke now, his voice low enough to be heard by no one else, yet carrying clearly and matter-of-factly to her. "You just have to check all you've believed in, don't you, for the period of the war?"

Instinct told her not to glance in his direction but to keep her curved hands coming together and together in the steady beat of the dance. "Check stubs get lost so easily. I like to carry my valuables along."

"But what if you aren't sure," he said slowly, "whether they are as valuable as you once thought?"

"Unimportant things wouldn't be worrying you so much, would they?"

The tap dancers were reaching an impressive height of speed. Through the crashing crescendo of the music she could barely hear his surprised, "Have you really got something there, lady?"

"Of course," she said calmly as though speaking to her own volatile, sensitive son and led the way to a momentarily deserted davenport.

"It's like this," he said lighting a cigarette and looking straight ahead. "Before I enlisted in the Air Force I went to see the minister in our small town about whether some things in the Bible were to be taken literally. I wasn't trying to show off. I wanted to know how he felt about it. But he said there was no problem to discuss and that I had no right to question what the Bible says."

"You felt he thought you had no reason for anxiety."

"That's right. But it's not so easy to know what it is the Bible says. What about this questioning business anyway? That's not wrong, is it?"

Renewed applause and the beginning of an encore filled the pause while she thought how best to answer him.

"I'll tell you one thing I'm sure is wrong. If a person does start questioning, if he breaks away from ways of thinking that don't seem real to him and starts to hew out a faith of his own, its wrong for him to stop until he has found answers that seem firm and sure to him."

"But people like you—gay, sophisticated and steady—have you found the answers?"

In the midst of all the noise and confusion around them something quiet within her was thankful she could answer that.

"Of course—all I need to go ahead on. You grow into it—the ability, I mean, to find the answers. And then you and this knowhow keep on growing together."

"Go on," he said.

"If what a person believes is to be really important to him—and what good is it otherwise?—it has to keep up with the rest of his development. And 'questioning', as you call it, may be a healthy sign of 'faith fretting at its outworn form'."

"Gosh, lady!" he said, slowly, "you don't know how that helps!"

He left her abruptly then. She saw him leave the club. And she knew that it was her being a stranger—and staying a stranger—that had made it possible for him to talk to her as he had.

Slowly she got up from the davenport. Only then did she observe two things at once: that it was after ten o'clock and that the sergeant straight across the building from her was still looking out of the library window. He had missed the last bus, there were no taxis to be had, and he was due back at midnight.

As she went a little wearily through the crowded lounge and hall and on into the library, she changed her mind twice about what she should say to him. You've missed your bus, was her first thought. Then, it's twenty-five miles down there to the Fort and you'll be AWOL if you don't make it.

But as she came up to him and he made no attempt to move away, she knew neither one would do. "Why is it so hard to go back?" she asked instead.

His voice didn't sound surprised, either that she was there or that she asked the question.

"I've just been let out of Officers' Training."

"What didn't measure up—your hearing or your eyes?"

The look he gave her was so grateful it hurt her. "Eyes. They thought at first they'd let me by. But they'll think back at the Fort I'm just bellyaching, that it was my fault, that I don't have what it takes."

Mrs. Morris said nothing. He must do this himself. She suspected he had been working it out all day without being aware of it. However, it took him several more long minutes to see it. Then he spoke so sharply she knew the true state of affairs had just dawned on him.

"But I don't have what it takes, do I? I'm proving they're right—"

She nodded. "But you're not AWOL—yet."

"You mean you'll drive me back?"

"Do you mean you're asking me to? Do you realize I've been on duty nearly fourteen hours already?" She meant to make it hard for him. She could see he was the kind of man who disliked to impose on people. She would make it clear that this would be an imposition. How else could she be sure he'd stay put in his resolve? If he didn't mean to pull himself together once and for all she was too tired to bother with him. This had already been a day beyond the average.

Then she realized that for the first time he was gazing at her steadily. "Yes," he was saying slowly, "you must have worked all of fourteen hours already. I saw you come into the club this morning. You must be dead. And your daughter's home too."

She could have told him that even if she drove him to the Fort she would be home before Harriet. But she mustn't make it easy for him. He must hate asking her.

"I do ask you," he said simply and for the first time that day she was sure of the quality of his strength.

Favorite Piece

Over and over went the same piece on the victrola until, what with the heat and me being muscle-bound from hauling the furniture out of the way of the wedding, I thought I'd scream if the sailor played it one more time. Not but what I liked the record well enough when they had played it soft through the ceremony an hour ago.

It'd been quite a day. I don't believe in whipped-up weddings if they can be avoided. When a boy asks if he can be married in the USO I know he's thinking it won't be quite so impersonal as the courthouse, the mayor's office, or maybe even an unfamiliar church. He wants it to look more planned, as though it were arranged just for him and his girl. A lot of hooey has been talked about the USO's being the boys' home-away-from-home. But the least you can do for a wedding is make one corner of the club look as intimate and friendly as possible. This one-armed sailor had been a big help today, shoving davenports around, lighting candles, all for a couple he didn't even know.

But when I saw he was winding the victrola up again, I said, "Haven't you sort of got that tune on the brain, son?"

"Oh sorry. It used to be my favorite piece."

I caught the bitterness in his eyes before he could cover up. For a moment I said nothing nor did he, though he stood his ground. Somehow I got the impression he didn't want the conversation to end just there.

"You're married," I said more or less at random.

"Yes."

I looked at his four service stripes. "Have you seen her since you came back?"

He shook his head, then fairly yelled at me, "I was reported missing. I'm going to stay that way, see?"

"I'm hungry," I said. "Guess I didn't eat anything at the wedding."

He came to the kitchen with me while I warmed the coffee. When I began on my second sandwich he gave up worrying his first one and said less loudly, "She has an antipathy for a person's being maimed. She told me so before I enlisted. But I joined up anyway. It was the only quarrel we ever had."

"She came around afterward, of course."

"She didn't take that part back. How could she when it was true? She did write me several wonderful letters, though—before I was reported missing." Then eagerly, "Want to see one?"

Printed across the top of the sheet were her name and address. I have an awful memory but I prayed I'd remember them.

Yes of course I called her up long distance as soon as I could get loose from the kid. I didn't pay any attention to all that stuff about minding your own business. There were too many lonely folks around those days, best you could do. I told her everything—about the arm not being there, and his staying missing, and the record that had almost driven me nuts.

"I can get there—to the club—by ten tomorrow night," she told me when her voice was making sense again.

I said I'd manage to have her husband handy.

"Look," she said, "could you do one more thing for us?"

"Sure," I said. I knew what she meant.

I put a fresh needle in the victrola ahead of time and gave the record a twirl when I saw her taxi stop.

It was just one good needle wasted, though. They never heard a note.

CHAPTER VI

All the World's a Stage

"*Picture a huge ship, sides rusty and peeling, tied to a dock. The wind* is blowing cold off Mt. Ballyhoo. Dutch Harbor is flecked with white-capped, restless waves. It will soon be time to sail and, in the meantime, no one is permitted off the ship. They have had no recreation; there has been nothing to do to break the monotony of the trip. Now they stand around idly, waiting for something to happen. It does.

"By happy coincidence, there are two traveling units of USO-Camp Shows in Dutch Harbor at that particular moment. One of them is an all-girl unit; the other is made up of two men and three girls. Since the men cannot come ashore to a show, then the show will come to the men. And in almost less time than it takes to tell it, an improvised stage is erected on the dock immediately in front of the ship, a loud speaker is hooked up to a microphone and the show is on.

"It was a thrilling sight. Every available inch of space aboard that ship was crowded with soldiers, each seeking a vantage point from which to see the show. They were lined several deep along the rail; they sat in the life boats and on the life rafts. I don't believe that any troupers ever played to a more appreciative audience than did those USO entertainers to the amusement-starved soldiers.

"The show proceeded: songs, instrumental solos, dances, jokes, imitations. Everything was running smoothly, with one of the men doing a turn at the mike. Suddenly an officer came up to him, there was a quick exchange of conversation and then the USO man announced, 'I have just been told that your ship is to shove off right now. But with your permission, we'll carry on the show just as long as you are within sight and hearing. Okay?'

"The roar of approval that went up from the ship left him in no doubt whatsoever. The show went on, from that point, against the background of noises of a ship getting under way, the shouted orders, the clank of chain, the creak of gangways.

"It came the turn of the two men together. They sang funny verses to the tune of "Hinkey-Dinkey Parlez Vous," and the soldiers joined lustily in the chorus across the ever-widening gap of water. They finished their number and the girl with the accordion took the microphone. Tugs were bustling about the ship and were nudging her out into the stream. Her nose was already turning. The girl at the mike sang song after song. Then she began, softly and warmly, to sing "Aloha." The voices of the men, joined with hers, drifted back across Dutch Harbor. The ship had turned; only her stern showed to us ashore. But we could hear the men singing as they sailed for Attu.

"The wind nipped across the dock. The girls in their thin stage costumes were red with cold. The men bundled them into coats. Another show was done. They would say, 'It's all in the day's work. We're glad to do it.'

"But I, who had stood by and had seen that show, knew it was more than that. A transport of men had been made happy by Camp Shows as they sailed away to war."

So wrote Chaplain Jacob Philip Rudin to a friend on July 7, 1943, while on duty in the Aleutian Islands. In his brief account are the purpose and meaning of USO-Camp Shows. Between this picture of the end result, however, and the beginning of the task, there is a period of meticulous planning involving organization on a gigantic scale. In a matter of months show business, rising to the emergency, expanded to encompass a world-wide stage.

It has been the biggest enterprise that American show business ever tackled. The audience was the millions of American fighting men; the stage was global; the producer was USO-Camp Shows. From behind the footlights of Broadway's theaters, from the concert hall and operatic stage, from the sound stages of Hollywood and the studios of radio networks, from vaudeville theaters, night clubs and dance floors came actors, concert artists, popular singers, comedians, dancers and novelty acts, orchestras and popular bands in answer to Camp Shows casting call. Names to conjure with in the Show World rubbed elbows and shared rations with youngsters balancing on the lower rungs of the entertainment ladder.

It all began in 1941, in the days when draft boards were still without filing cabinets and calling low numbers. The War Department had asked that a Citizen's Committee assist in supplying entertainment within training camps. By means of seven traveling show buses, more than 3,200,000 men were entertained during that summer, but the arrangement, sponsored and made possible by public minded citizens, proved inadequate to take care of the growing entertainment needs of the ever-increasing ranks of khaki and navy blue.

In the autumn of 1941, the Citizen's Committee, the USO and representatives of show business met in Washington. As a result of that meeting, USO-Camp Shows was formed and designated by the War and Navy Departments as Official Entertainer to the men and women of the armed forces.

The assignment to a civilian organization of such an important responsibility was made after full consideration by the War and Navy Departments. The Army and Navy wanted its men and women to have a time and a place free of regimentation. It was felt that the entertainment program should be signally without the formality and the necessary discipline of other phases of service life; that it should be a link with home and that it would be stronger if it were forged by a citizen organization.

And it was a link with home. The men and women of the armed

forces came from every walk of life and from every hamlet, village, town and city in the country. So did the Camp Show entertainers and, in addition, the vagaries and wanderings of theatrical life made them familiar with hundreds of towns and villages other than their own. Wherever they went through all the ramifications of this war of vast distances, they met boys from home who, for a few minutes of unadulterated delight, could talk of names and places to someone who understood.

The most famous circuit of USO-Camp Shows, the Foxhole Circuit was pioneered by a courageous group of stage and screen performers who blazed the trail for future troupers of the GI stages around the world. On November 1, 1941, this unit climbed aboard a B-18 transport christened "The Flying Showboat" and followed a 13,000-mile circuit through the Caribbean—from Puerto Rico to British Guiana—bringing entertainment to troops all along the way. They were Overseas Unit No. 1, and they proved beyond a doubt that show business could and would follow the troops wherever they were sent. The eager, heartwarming reception which the soldier audiences gave Overseas Unit No. 1 was an indication of how great the need was for the morale-building assistance of the entertainment world.

Promptly four additional units went out to Newfoundland and other Arctic points. Within five months, thirty-eight units had been supplied to Bermuda, Iceland, Newfoundland, Great Britain and Panama, and the first troupe had beaten its way to Australia.

On December 22, 1942, fifteen entertainers boarded a plane from New York for South Pacific headquarters. Two months later, ten performers flew to the Middle East. By spring, 1943, 119 overseas units were delivered.

Broadway was transported to the battlefield—within the sound of guns, as near to the boy in the front line as the military authorities would allow. On his fourth trip overseas a headline movie actor wrote: "We have been out of San Francisco fifteen days and have done 38 shows and visited six hospitals. Couldn't sleep last night because four of the big guns were firing every ten minutes all night, just 150 yards away from us."

Amid the terrible uncertainties of his life, the American soldier spent a nostalgic hour laughing at jokes—American brand, listening to music—American style, looking at pretty girls, like no other pretty girls in the world—American girls, as USO-Camp Shows carried forward its far-flung program to all the theaters of war.

Typical of the gratitude which the men felt for the entertainment is this letter, written from a soldier in Northern Burma to his mother, on October 31, 1944:

"Dear Mom:

"In this letter, I had intended to tell you about the country itself, but I'm sure you could find it all in some geography book. Instead, I shall include what you might call an editorial which I wrote several nights ago, after seeing a USO-Camp Show.

OPEN LETTER TO THE USO

'Last night, for the first time in a long time, the men here in Northern Burma were satisfied; satisfied to the extent that they hit the hay, practically normal humans once more. What caused this magical change in temperament? What converted these mechanical men into flesh and blood? The answer is found in just three letters—USO!

'Through the medium of a traveling Camp Show, five girls put laughter and memories into the hearts of nearly 500 lonely GIs— GIs who haven't seen a beautiful American girl in two years, some cases longer.

'A mighty spontaneous roar went up when the girls pranced on the stage. The men clapped and stamped; yelled and screamed; howled and whistled. The din was terrific—months of pent-up emotion blew out in one instant.

'The girls sang, danced, teased the boys—and made them like it. Every song, every word called for more screams and howls. No—it wasn't a Broadway musical; no famous names appeared

USO's Inside and Outside Continental United States

Morning—Noon, and Night—the Same Day

Serving Religious Needs

Games—Group and Individual

Sharing a Letter from Home

The Art of Finger Painting

Competition with Checkers
and with Water Pistols

Showing Servicemen How to Make Jewelry from Shells

Nurses Learn to Weave

All Americans Are Welcome

Facilities for Music

Off-duty Lunch

Service to Negroes

Dancing—Formal and Square

With Convalescents

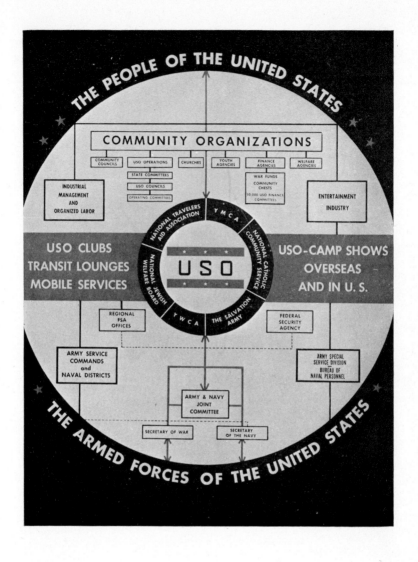

Mobile Service

USO Camp Shows

Watching USO Entertainers

on the marquee—and the orchestra was just a bunch of fellows who had gotten together for the occasion. But, be that as it may, to these men who have suffered intolerable tortures from Mother Nature and the Japs—it was a miracle—a temporary Shangri-La—where their cares and worries could be dispersed. No greater play or musical received such an ovation. A half hour after the performance the men were still sitting in the rain, still applauding...

'So to these five girls, and all like them—and to the USO-Camp Shows, which made it possible, I say thanks. Thanks for doing a swell job. I only hope that there are more at home like you! HM!'

"That finished the editorial and also this letter—I hope everyone at home is feeling fine—as for me, I never felt better in my life—so, till the next time—all my love to the family.

Your son,
Harold"

Another GI wrote from North Africa to his wife, on July 14, 1944, giving a vivid word-picture of a performance by a violinist whose name is known around the world, an artist who helped bring Carnegie Hall to the Beachheads and the outposts of war. He wrote:

"After playing The Star Spangled Banner, the Master himself introduced his first number,—Prelude by Bach. In a very serious tone he said: 'In musical language this is spinach. Whether you like it or not—it's good for you.'

"When he said the formal program was over, and asked what we would like to hear, practically everyone in the place called for something, so my request for a portion of the Bruch Concerto was drowned in the din.

" 'What, no Bumble Bee?' said the Master.

"Then he said the next number was on the house. Written for a 'hot fiddle' it is called In The Groove. A master is a master and he made it sound like something hot and sacred at the same time. . . . Applause followed his last number for 10 minutes. As for me, the experience made the trip to Africa worthwhile.

"During the concert, there was a constant din set up by the roar of airplane motors just outside, but few were bothered by it, the 'temperamental' artist least of all. His only comment was: 'I seem to have some competition.' "

In the spring of 1944 while our troops waited on the British side of the Channel for the invasion order, Camp Shows toured the tent cities located in the fields and on the beaches. For these performers July 28 was D-Day when eight Camp Shows units landed on Utah Beach. Plywood was laid down on a 30-ton ammunition carrier. A public address system was set up. Two hours after landing the show was on for men who had been living in foxholes for forty-eight days. Some walked miles through sand to see it.

Next day each of the eight units was off on its own. Army Special Service Officers rounded up enough pyramidal tents and cots to go around making the Camp Shows units completely mobile, able to move forward on command.

Already Camp Shows had rung up many a curtain in North Africa, Sicily and Italy. Now they flowed into fortress Europe wherever and whenever possible. A radio reporter took his mike to the front line to describe by short wave what he found there in October of 1944: "There were cheers and whistles and loud laughter coming from a building and that was a mighty good thing to hear in this section of the front, just east of Aachen. I investigated and saw a sign reading, 'Girls' Dressing Room.' This then was the real thing—a show with girls in it. Standing guard by the door was a soldier I recognized. The last time I had seen him he was shooting Germans. He told me how his boys had been given a few days' rest and this show was part of the treatment.

"I watched from the wings as a girl in a ballet costume did cartwheels and flips, and every turn brought applause and cheers. Then the magician performed and his assistant was another pretty girl, thinly clad in an evening dress, and the magician was Master of Ceremonies too. Then a girl singer came on the stage, and she was a good singer—a comic singer in the style of the 'Gay 90s'. . . .

"As the performers went through their acts, the happy sparkle in the soldiers' eyes eased into crinkles and then the crinkles broke into broad grins and the grins into howling guffaws of enjoyment, and for an hour and fifteen minutes that little old building just rocked with fun and hilarity at this USO show . . . played to American soldiers taking a rest in the shadow of the Siegfried Line.

"For five weeks now these performers have been playing here in Germany, right in the front-line area. Sometimes they live out of trucks and tents and put their make-up on in a muddy field under an apple tree. Other times they live in houses—broken houses with no windows and sometimes the house next to them gets hit by enemy shell fire. And like everybody at the front, they go hunting in the neighboring cabbage patch for a change of diet.

"They may not be the biggest names in show business back home, but they're headliners here, and if you could see the faces of GIs watching their performance, you would see why."

The Camp Shows Hospital Sketching Artists program probably came closest of all to the men who made up our fighting forces. Some thirty thousand portraits of wounded servicemen, drawn by one hundred and seventy leading illustrators and portrait artists in hospitals here and overseas, provided what is probably the most comforting kind of happiness for the soldier and his family who received the portrait. For them, it will be an eternal reminder of a USO-Camp Shows service.

One father wrote: "I am writing in most grateful appreciation of the sketch of our son done on November 27th in England. Surely I can testify to the value of this project. The sketch was the last thing we ever received from our son. He died in a U.S. Army Hospital in England on December 5th, 1944. From the bottom of our hearts we thank the USO for the portrait—it will be a source of great comfort to us in the years that lie ahead."

Both the great and the small of show business gave unstintingly during those troubled years. A galaxy of big names that no theatrical circuit in the history of entertainment could hope to match gave generously of their talent to Camp Shows. But these were only a small part of those beneath the Camp Shows banner. The more than 5,000 salaried performers came from every classification among the meanderings of show business. There were singers, jugglers and gymnasts, magicians and fresh youngsters from the chorus lines of famous musicals and theaters. There were athletes, boxers, wrestlers, fencers, and fly fishermen, concert artists, comedians and puppetteers. There were youngsters and oldsters but they were all alike in their willingness to do their best under any conditions, wherever they were able.

A columnist whose knowledge of people has made him loved and respected by the American reading public, took these Camp Shows troupers to his heart. "The greatest morale job of the war," he said, "was done by what I could call the little people of show business did I not loathe the term little people. Let me speak of them rather as the unsung.

"They are the performers of the stage and the night clubs and the screen of less reputation than the headliners. They moved about the war areas, not for a few months but for several years, presenting their acts for the entertainment of our fighting men. You did not hear much of them.

"You heard of . . . the stars. They too, journeyed to far places to entertain the soldiers and sailors and Marines. They too, did a fine job. I am not detracting from their efforts one whit, as the saying is.

"They did grand work, these top notchers, no doubt of that. But I think the unsung did even grander work and under more adverse conditions."

Enroute to England, where he was to serve as war correspondent, a well-known novelist also wrote of them:

"A small USO-Camp Shows unit is aboard this troopship, girls and men who are going out to entertain troops wherever they may be sent.

These are not the big names who go out with blasts of publicity and maintain their radio contracts. These are girls who can sing and dance and look pretty, and men who can do magic, pantomimists and tellers of jokes. They have few properties and none of the tricks of light and color that dress up the theater. But there is something very gallant about them. The spirit must be high. This is trouping the really hard way."

Camp Shows turned to the sports world, as it had to show business, and met with enthusiastic response. Leaders in their fields banded themselves into units and joined the circuit. Big-game fishermen gathered audiences out of the mud and smoke of the Italian front and told tales of ocean battles with deep sea denizens. A gallant veteran of forty years of wrestling worked in France and Belgium, and other experts played table tennis with the boys in the postage-stamp fields of Normandy.

Not a single branch of sport has fallen down. Baseball headliners were scheduled for one night stands through New Guinea jungles and they then trouped around the world to tell servicemen how their favorite ball clubs were going. Others toured the European Theater of Operations with stories of ring activities or played exhibition tennis in the Caribbean stations. Bowling and badminton stars entertained in the fog and snow of Alaska and the Aleutians. Also generously on tour for Camp Shows were umpires and sports writers.

USO-Camp Shows has presented entertainment in 41 foreign countries, areas and continents: Alaska, Alcan Highway, Australia, Bermuda, Brazil, Belgium, British Isles, Burma, Canada, Caribbean, Central Africa, Central Pacific, China, Egypt, France, Greece, Greenland, Germany, Hawaii, Iceland, India, Iran, Iraq, Italy, Labrador, Malta, Netherlands, New Caledonia, Newfoundland, North Africa, Panama, Persian Gulf, Peru, Philippines, Sardinia, Sicily, South America, South Pacific, Southwest Pacific, Venezuela, West Africa.

In addition to service overseas, three circuits have operated in continental United States: the Victory Circuit, entertaining at Army posts and camps and Naval stations with a troop population of 1,500 or more; the Blue Circuit, playing in tabloid units consisting of five variety entertainers capable of putting on a show indoors or out before 15 men or 1,500; the Hospital Circuit, inaugurated in March, 1944.

The excitement of following the troops behind the moving war fronts made day-to-day living of USO-Camp Shows entertainers a saga of adventure long to be remembered.

One of America's most popular screen and radio stars with his Camp Shows company entertained as close as 1,000 yards to the front and once they almost lost their entire audience to the Germans. "We were doing a show in a captured aircraft factory when the Germans counter-attacked," came the report. "I'd have to keep interrupting the show to make announcements—'Will such and such a platoon meet the Lieutenant at the back door—Will such and such a platoon meet Lieutenant So and So at the front door.'

"I gradually talked myself out of an audience. The grim thing about it is that when I met four or five hundred of them the next day at an evacuation hospital, they demanded I continue the show at the point they'd had to leave."

He stayed behind his unit at one place in the Metz area "to hear the padre say Mass", and a lieutenant offered to drive him back to the ack-ack battery where the unit was to go after Mass.

"We batted along in the jeep," he reported later, "and all of a sudden I noticed we'd run out of telephone wire. (The wire along the road is a sure sign some other Allied soldiers have been there first.) Then we came to a town and I noticed the name—it was one I'd seen on the war maps that morning as being in German hands!

"I turned to the Lieutenant. 'Do you know where we are?' I shouted.

" 'Nope, I'm afraid I'm lost.'

" 'Lieutenant, do me a favor? Turn this thing around and let's get the blazes out of here!' "

That evening this headline entertainer had dinner with the Commanding Officer.

"Where've you been today?" he asked his guest conversationally. He was told. "But that's in German hands!"

"We had it for two minutes, sir!"

Somewhere in France, a popular singer and her troupe were giving a show when trucks began to roar by, jam-packed with thousands of German prisoners. The spectacle stopped the show cold, and the master of ceremonies yelled out, "Fellas, there's the greatest show in the world. We can't top that!"

At another point the same show performed for a large audience under the cover of Ninth Air Force planes which were protecting them. Around the audience antiaircraft guns were installed and during the show, a German plane was brought down.

Near the Seine, engineers built a bridge and named it after this same star. They called on her to christen it and after the ceremony she sang for them. It was only after the show was over that they discovered a German sniper had been sitting in a nearby tree, watching the whole proceedings through his gunsights. Immediately after the show he surrendered!

A popular trio of sisters had their share of adventures overseas. When they landed in Casablanca they set a record of ten performances in two-and-a-half days, before their scheduled tour had really begun! It was there, walking down the street on their second day, that a jeep pulled alongside and a sergeant told them that they were wanted at headquarters. Without questions, they jumped in and found themselves being driven miles into the country. When the jeep finally stopped, they were in a remote army installation with hundreds of soldiers who had never seen a USO-Camp Show. They were told that they'd been kidnapped and a command performance was in order.

The eagerness and appreciation with which entertainment-starved GIs received Camp Shows troupers everywhere was deeply touching. Hospitalized servicemen at Oahu resorted to practical strategy to show their approval of a quartet of girl musicians who had been playing there. In order to delay the girls' departure for Saipan, they disassembled the musicians' music stands, then hid the pieces under mattresses and inside plaster casts.

On Bougainville, a dancer tapped out rhythms with her twinkling feet and enjoyed the distinction of being the only white woman on the island for more than a month! Several thousand Seabees gave her a scroll inscribed to "The White Goddess of Bougainville."

Nor were Camp Shows admirers always masculine. A young specialty dancer, who stayed overseas touring for Camp Shows for almost two years before coming home, struck up a friendship with a group of Army nurses at one installation. Changing her clothes in their tent after the performance, they begged her to stay over for a few days. She replied that she couldn't because she had to keep her show schedule. The nurses were dismayed. "Why you *can't* leave," they said. "We've already dug your foxhole for you!"

One evening a male comedian who was in one of the first units covering the European Theater, was playing at an airfield in Britain. A group of American flyers were about to go out on a bombing mission. They asked him if he could hold up the show until they got back. He said "Sure" and took his troupe down to the control tower to wait for the men to return. It was a pretty tough night over Germany but through the ack-ack, weaving in and out of the Messerschmitts, one pilot found time to radio a message to another pilot in the air and the message came through to the control tower where the troupe waited. It said: "Wonder if they'll hold up that Camp Show until we get back?"

Nor was appreciation lacking for the kind of individual who wore the Camp Shows uniform. One evening a girl was singing for soldiers in a great theater in Naples. She had finished her numbers and was making a little speech, telling the men she hoped she had been able to bring them the spirit of their sweethearts, wives and mothers. In the midst of this the door opened and down the aisle came a tall blond GI.

He was covered with mud. His helmet and gun were slung over his shoulder and his face was still grim from battle.

He walked up to the stage and listened to her for a minute, watching her intently. Then he said, "I'd like to say something," and climbed up on the stage. He took hold of the mike and looked at her. She had her eyes on the ground afraid of what he might say. "I've got to contradict you," he said. "You don't look like anyone's sweetheart. You don't look like anyone's wife. And God knows you don't look like anyone's mother." Then he lifted her chin up and she saw the tears on his cheeks. He kissed her on the forehead. "You look like an angel," he said. And he turned around and marched out of the theater.

That was the first time she cried. And, some said, there wasn't a soldier in the house who didn't have his handkerchief out.

Many Camp Shows entertainers have been generous in assisting chaplains with their services at posts where the units were entertaining. Such a trouper was the popular official Mother to the 75th Seabees on Samar Island. She was fifty-eight and white-haired when she started on a tour of the Pacific Area in 1944 for Camp Shows. She played character parts and took the steaming heat, the tropical rains, the rough conditions of travel and of daily living like any other trouper.

With her smile and her white hair, she became "Mom" to every GI she met. The 75th Seabees were so taken with her, they begged her to come back to their station at Calicoan for Mother's Day, 1945. She went, and this is her description of the occasion:

"They met me with a big corsage of oleanders tied up with gilt paper and ribbon. I attended Protestant, Catholic and Jewish services with the boys. They were all in the same chapel—that's what impressed me. At the Protestant services, they asked me to read the Scriptures. So, I read that one from Corinthians—all about charity. Oh, what a lump came in my throat!"

At the end of the day, they gave her a folder, inscribed, "To 'Mom' ——————, the grandest girl in the world."

A sailor in the Aleutian Islands wrote this letter to Camp Shows:

"It was Christmas Eve and as we sat in church waiting for the services to begin, the Chaplain stood before the congregation and said 'Men, we are waiting for a group of five girls from USO troupe, rather, Unit #368, and I'm sure that they will indeed add enjoyment to our services for this evening.'

"Indeed they did, too, for when the girls came on the stage and began to play, it seemed that a tenseness went out of the air and each man relaxed within himself, for here indeed, was truly beautiful, smooth, restful music. As one of them sang, "Ave Maria", accompanied by another on the electric organ while a third played the violin, every heart and mind was flooded with the warmth and tenderness of her soft, clear voice. I could not refrain from shedding a tear, I know not why, but my heart was deeply touched and I was so glad that I had come to church on this evening for I was enjoying something that brought me closer to home and my loved ones than anything or anyone I have ever seen, or heard, in the eighteen months I have been here.

"A personal word about the ladies. I had the opportunity to meet them myself and they were more than happy to talk to the enlisted men. Their friendly, wholesome personalities, their enthusiastic answers to questions too, all added up to the typical American girl and by gosh, mister, that means a lot to us.

"I'm not implying that the other girls who have come up here are not just that, for we have had the grandest entertainment in the world. It's just that these girls are simply swell, and it is our earnest hope, plea, desire that you send them, or a troupe just like them, along to us again soon."

A well known male comedian who holds one of the longest Camp Shows' records for overseas trouping, is the possessor of an eloquent letter of thanks, written on March 15, 1945, by a chaplain of the Ninth Army:

"I want to make this letter just as informal and sincere as your splendid address to us chaplains at Maestricht some weeks ago was.

"Last Saturday, our battalion had the privilege of seeing one of the USO-Camp Shows units, which operated out of your headquarters. I can say truthfully that it was the best production I have seen in more than two years' overseas service. For more than one hour, hundreds of soldiers were doubled up with laughter. The show never lagged. There were no dull moments; it was just swell. But, here's the point I want to bring out: There was no dirt, filth, sex or cursing in it. Every soldier must have noticed that also yet every soldier praises the show as highly as I do. This proves that clean shows can be entertaining to the *n*th degree.

"For myself and many others, I wish to thank whatever persons in your command supervise these activities for sending us such fine entertainment. They, and the cast, deserve a pat on the back.

"May God continue to bless you and the Ninth Army in which we serve with honour, and, I hope, distinction."

One of the earliest entertainers on the Foxhole Circuit was a singer of whom a clergyman wrote, after meeting her in Florence during the war, "She was the toast of the Fifth Army. She gave special programs in the hospitals, and the chaplains told me that she crowded her Sundays with chapel appearances—hers is a golden voice for hymns."

One day she visited a hospital near Anzio, filled with the casualties from the fierce fighting still raging on the Italian coastal plain. She was walking through the wards, singing without accompaniment *"Ave Maria," "I Love You Truly"* and other songs the men had heard at home. Soldiers called to her, asking her to sing their favorites, which she did.

From a bed in a corner came a voice less strong than the others. When she approached she saw a red-headed youngster who managed a smile and the whispered question, would she sing one song for him. She said of course she would. What was the song?

It was a moment before he could put into words that he hadn't many more hours to live. "I want you to sing '*Abide With Me*' at my funeral."

Quickly she assured him that his request was many years premature—that he wasn't going to die—that he was going to get well—

He seemed not to hear. "Promise. Please."

"I promise," she said quietly.

Two days later she stood in a heavy downpour beside the youngster's grave. As the chaplain finished intoning the simple service, she kept her promise and *"Abide With Me"* rose clear, if not steady, above the sound of the rain.

How the USO-Camp Shows' job looks to the entertainers themselves has been ably described in several books. Their attitude may be indicated by the following excerpts from a letter written from New Guinea on one of the war Thanksgiving Days by a Camp Shows Trouper:

"Dear People: Here but a few degrees from the Equator it is, if I may say so, very warm for Thanksgiving. But climate notwithstanding, turkey and all the home fixin's taste just as good or better than usual, as can be attested to by the fact that I'm distributing myself over three Thanksgiving dinners today.

"To those of you who are interested, I have never had less sleep, never felt healthier, certainly never happier, and certainly never so full of respect, admiration, and pride in my fellow Americans, that walk this part of the earth. For that jaded faith in human kind, the best thing I could wish anyone is a trip to the Southwest Pacific Theater of War. . . .

"To go 'way back three short months ago—on my birthday, to be exact—we waved farewell to the Golden Gate for a destination unknown to any of us. 'Now it can be told' we traveled in a Dutch merchant ship, the Dutch crew of which left their homes five years ago for what was supposed to be their routine run from the Netherlands to Cape Town. They were shunted to the South

Pacific and haven't seen their homes since. Many of them know they may no longer have homes. It's a fairly small ship—a combination luxury liner and troopship.

"One other USO unit—a concert troupe of 2 men and 3 girls—was aboard. If you think life for six girls among so many men is hard to take, try it some time, you gals. Here we got our first taste of the unprecedented popularity which has been ours in this man's world—and which, I'm afraid, has spoiled us forever for back home, where the man-woman ratio works the other way. But here, too, almost unconsciously, one sets a course of policy, as it were, to guide one in the topsy-turvy social scheme of one girl to thousands of men. . . .

"Days began at sunrise and ended whenever you could tear yourself away from that last look at the Pacific sky, so unbelievably covered with stars. But they were never long enough to do all the 'fun' things that as grand a bunch of men as ever lived could find for you to do. Perhaps the shortest way and the only way to tell it is simply to list a series of unforgettable impressions: the dense black-out to which you became so accustomed that on a night when someone forgot and lit a cigarette, it took on all the proportions of a burning sky-scraper. Playing the show (we did it three times) on the open deck with the wind blowing you about and the deck heaving under your feet; the evening song fests when hundreds of fine, strong men's voices thrilled you more than any concert ever will. The church services in the men's mess . . . closing with a prayer that choked you—not because it was a very good prayer, but because you knew what every man prayed for.

"Neptune Day—the crossing of the Equator—and the fabulous ceremony that attended it (curtailed a bit because there's a war on and also because there were six women aboard), where men were 'spotted' by the Royal Family for head shaving, rotten egg baths and dunking in an improvised pool and where all 6 girls were royally dunked, too. That night when, as a gesture of feminine protest, we wore dinner dresses, only to find that that night was the first of the evening stand-to's and the first gas mask drill, and at sunset we stood for fifty minutes in long dresses, topped by

Mae Wests, and for part of the time, grotesque gas masks. . . .

"The day the first plane was sighted, general quarters called, the gun crew rushed to man the guns, the plane was recognized as friendly and a half relieved, half excited shout went up from all hands. The first rain, when the troops on the deck below soaped themselves to the waist, only to have the shower stop. . . .

"The first glimpse of our destination, the long thrilling process of landing, the first native fuzzy-wuzzie (kinky hair dyed yellow with peroxide—they'd give you New Guinea for a bottle of it) and our first sight of an American Army base in a beautiful land that you'd scarcely heard of before the war, but which was to become the site of a nearly 3 year long battle and the lonely home of thousands and thousands of American men. The gang plank and your feet on land again after 3 weeks of a ship's deck. The first cocoanuts, presented to me by dozens of GIs hungry for the sight of someone fresh from the States. . . .

"Our first stop in New Guinea found us (the three girls) situated with the Red Cross girls—in barracks that shot up almost overnight like a mushroom to house us, sharing one shower, one latrine and one ironing board, with some 80 girls. In a day we dropped all hope of privacy. We were in the Army! Here those sharp uniforms issued us by the USO and the colored cotton dresses we'd been told to buy in great numbers were literally torn from our backs and we were poured into GI trousers and shirts (sleeves rolled down) and flat heeled nurses shoes—standard garb for health reasons and general practicability throughout this theater of war. . . .

"Since this first base, we have traveled by C-47s from one end of New Guinea to the other with a split week in New Britain. We've been quartered in hospitals with board walls and floors, or with Nipa walls and no floors; in a PT base in a specially constructed tent, complete with hot and cold running water, surrounded by a stockade and protected by an armed guard. Now we find ourselves in a pyramidal tent among the Wacs, sole furnishings of which are 3 Army cots, *sans* mattresses, *sans* pillows, *sans* sheets. But we're still a long way from a foxhole.

"Since that first day in New Guinea, I've eaten C Rations and I've eaten steak and ice-cream—dehydrated potatoes and eggs and the ever present spam and bullybeef, and I've drunk unforgettable glasses of milk flown in from Australia. Life is cheap in New Guinea as compared to a glass of milk and a green salad. I've stood in chow lines handling my mess gear with the best of them and I've eaten in mess halls far more picturesque than any atmospheric job in New York City.

"I've ridden in and driven jeeps, peeps, weapons' carriers, command cars, tanks, ducks, M8s and LSTVs. I've flown in an Aussie bomber on a mission over Jap held territory. I've flown in P-38s, A-20s and Piper Cubs. I've broadcast from a jungle radio station. . . . I've been wakened in the middle of the night by a rat scampering across my face. . . I've tramped through the jungle, cutting our way with a machette (never understanding how men can fight an enemy through it when I can scarcely walk through it); I've stood in mud up to my ankles with the dust blowing thick around my head. . . .

"All this is on the 'fun' side, but believe me, the work is even more thrilling and soul satisfying. We're driven in jeeps and command cars anywhere from 5 miles to 30, bouncing over the rough roads in a cloud of black dust or red dust, as the case may be, so thick the driver can scarcely see the way or through a downpour so wet he can scarcely stay on the road. We learned what the GI meant by 'Oh, my aching back!' Now we're immune to even black and blue spots. We've played in 'theaters' that were only a board platform and the rest was left to our stage manager and his detail of GIs. We've dressed in tents in mud to our ankles and we've dressed in dressing rooms graced with the now familiar parachute ceiling and a real, though hastily constructed, dressing table. And often there were flowers in our dressing rooms!

"We've played to audiences, many of them, ankle deep in mud, huddled under their ponchos in the pouring rain (it breaks your heart the first two or three times to see men so hungry for entertainment). We've played on uncovered stages, when we, as well as the audience, got rain soaked. We've played with huge tropical

bugs flying in our hair and faces; we've played to audiences of
thousands of men, audiences spreading from our very feet to far
up a hillside and many sitting in the trees (last night two native
children sat perched throughout the performance on a corner of
the stage. How much they understood, I don't know, but they
laughed and clapped like crazy). We've played with a tropical
moon shining through the palm trees full in our faces.

"We've played to audiences in small units of 500 or so, and
much oftener to audiences of 8 to 10,000. Every night we play in
a different place. Certain audience cracks have become an accepted part of the show—we wait for them. Wisecracks are frequent but always friendly and they've long since ceased to faze
us. If GI Joe wants to enjoy a show that way, let him. Quicker to
resent him are his fellows if he gets too exuberant. Twenty-five
miles in blinding dust is small price to pay for the yells of laughter and the roars of applause that have definitely spoiled us for a
New York or a Chicago audience.

"But don't ever fool yourself that the GI audience in the Southwest Pacific, hungry for entertainment as it is, is not a discriminating and a smart one. Don't let yourself slip. Don't try to fool
a GI with a Hollywood face and very little talent; above all, don't
underestimate him by thinking all he wants is a leg show and
dirty cracks. He talks and listens to 'men' talk day in and day out.
Every woman back home wears a halo now and those who represent her had better keep theirs on too. *I've heard a girl swear out
here and sensed a roomful of men freeze for a second*. Give them
laughs, but see that they are good laughs. Give them plays. They
love them—from Tom of Arkansas, who's never seen one, to
Harry from New York who was brought up on Broadway.

"And the gratitude of them to you for coming out here is as
pathetic as it is undeserved and embarrassing. . . . USO work in
the South Pacific is Fun. And it is just as true in a sense that USO
fun is work. Not really, but it is the social life so eagerly supplied
by masculine New Guinea that can really knock you out if you
don't take a day off now and then for 'sack duty,' just to catch up.
A very important part of the work and fun is trying to be with

the enlisted men as much as possible. . . . Their appreciation is again embarrassing when you mess with them instead of with the officers or when you meet them in their recreation halls, wherever they have them. . . .

"And the hospitals. I can neither sing nor dance for the men. Often we cannot, because of the lack of facilities, play for hospitals, but difficult as it is at first, every visit to a hospital ward just to talk is maybe the finest thing you can do out here. . . .

"In hospitals or out, with everyone from a three star general to Pvt. Pete, the conversation begins with an invariable pattern 'Where are you from? How long have you been here? How do you like New Guinea?' . . . . and then, 'What's it like back in the States? Do they know there's a war out here?' And you try to tell them. But the real telling will come with what we do for them and with them when they're home once more. . . .

"They've fought a battle against the jungle, the climate, disease and perhaps worst of all, monotony. . . . These men have faced realities—the hard, cold facts of a comfortless existence and they're going to be sharp to penetrate the camouflage of flowery words and vague promises. And I think the toughest job of the home front is that of doing all we can to make our political and social scheme come up to our fighting men's ideal of America. They're not complaining now—not bitterly, that is (a certain amount of griping is part of the Army game)—and there's not one that doesn't say 'It's the boys in Europe or the boys up the line that are really taking it on the chin.'

"The good old American sense of humor is still functioning and strong. That's the eternal wonder of them, that makes you so proud of them you could 'bust.' They don't wave flags, they don't talk about the ideals they're fighting for. It has resolved itself into a job to do. They fight because the guy in the next foxhole fights. They kill because they've seen their buddies killed. But the home land to return to—the ultimate goal of all they've been through— had better be worth it when they get back. And they can't be fooled.

"With which sermon I'd better begin to draw to a close. . . .

I hope some of you write, but if you haven't time for everybody, and you know someone out here, write to him instead."

By the end of 1945, Camp Shows artists had performed in every area where our troops were stationed, from the lonely outposts on the Arctic Circle to lands along the Equator, at places that were once strange names on a map, but which became household words by the war's end.

The growth of the Camp Shows program has been commensurate with its rapidly mounting responsibilities to the fighting forces engaged in global war. In its first six months of operation, beginning in 1941, Camp Shows furnished a total of twenty-four units which gave 3,791 performances to camp audiences totalling 2,217,968 men. During 1945 Camp Shows artists gave 151,153 performances to an all-over-the-world audience of 71,968,363 servicemen and women. At the end of the year, in the overseas area alone, Camp Shows had 199 units and 1,522 artists furnishing entertainment to occupation-bound troops. Since its inception and up to the end of 1945 the complete Camp Shows audience totalled 171,717,205, the result of 273,599 separate visits of Camp Shows units to servicemen overseas and in the United States.

Traveling for USO-Camp Shows about the world brings much to the entertainer, aside from the lift he receives from entertaining the troops. There is a camaraderie, an *esprit de corps* among the "Soldiers in Greasepaint," as loyal and as indefinable as that of the GIs themselves. And nowhere is this spirit more evident than in the various USO-Camp Shows headquarters overseas.

The quiet little town of Chatou, a suburb of Paris, was the staging area for Camp Shows artists in Europe. On his most recent tour of the European Theater, one of America's outstanding comedians wrote back about walking into USO-Camp Shows headquarters there: "There are so many actors here the breeze from the bowing keeps the place air-conditioned! But it's wonderful. Regardless of your theatrical rating, everybody wears the same sort of uniform and stands in the same chow lines."

As the American troops took up their stations in Germany, and most of the men were evacuated from France, Camp Shows moved its European staging area from Chatou to Bad Schwalbach, Germany.

Shortly after the occupation of Japan, the Camp Shows staging areas in the Pacific were augmented by one in Tokyo. A columnist wrote a description of the Manila headquarters: "Since Barnum's museum on a rainy holiday, there has been nothing to compare with the Camp Shows staging area in Manila. Here groups of entertainers are assembled and dispatched to Japan, Korea and other troop centers in the Philippines and outlying Pacific Island areas.

"The staging area is a small palm-thatched community on the outskirts of the city. From dawn to dusk, it presents this picture: On the wooden-floored mess hall a row of chorus girls in slacks soft shoe through their routine to keep the pianist straight on his rhythm. . . . Across the way, comes the thump of drums and the moan of clarinets as a small band joggles lazily through its numbers. Over by the post exchange, an actress and the boys swap experiences."

So much for some of the things that go on in front of the Camp Shows banner. What happens behind it is another story. In the simplest terms, Camp Shows' job is to bring Hollywood and Broadway to the servicemen. This assignment has resulted in its being the largest theatrical enterprise in the world. Overseas entertainment is supplied by USO-Camp Shows only upon the request of the War and Navy Departments. A typical requisition during the combat period read: "Immediately, 5 people, mixed, male and female,—with star, if possible. Accordionist essential. Tropical climate, 6 months."

About six weeks after receiving such an order, Camp Shows will have its company collected, briefed, inoculated, and on the alert awaiting embarkation. During this interim six-week period, a mountain of detail will have been surmounted in preparing the acts for presentation. Casting calls will have been sent out, auditions held, endless hours spent in rehearsals. Every line must carry its proper punch; every gesture must be smooth and finished, for the GI audiences are as discriminating as any first-night crowd on Broadway, and only the best will succeed in entertaining them. Infinite care is given to costuming and scenery. Technicians check all mechanical problems. The transportation of scenery on a global scale calls for an entirely new technique in creating props and backgrounds and ingenious methods are worked out by the Camp Shows staff. Before the unit is sent overseas, the play or revue is performed before local service audiences, and the final, or polishing touches are added.

The show is reviewed by the Army's Special Service Division (Entertainment Branch). Vulgarisms, double entendres, and references to race, color and creed are not permitted. When the script has been approved, it cannot, under the regulations, be altered during the tour. Occasionally, a script has been departed from. When on rare occasions proof of improper behavior in changing a script has been clear, the guilty performer has been promptly ordered home.

In the preparation period, a feverish activity in the overseas-transportation department of Camp Shows centers about the departing unit. Passports must be obtained for each individual, and all War and State Department details arranged. Contracts must be drawn up, uniforms fitted, complete physical examinations given and inoculation certificates issued. In the publicity department, a similar routine of work is carried out in connection with the unit. Press books are written up, describing the presentation and each member of the cast, and photographs are made. These books and photographs as advance publicity material, are furnished the Army and Navy for distribution to areas to be visited by the entertainers.

Sailing orders may come at any time, and when they do the entertainers become, for all practical purposes, Army and Navy property. Their food, sleeping accommodations and audiences are provided by the Services and the unit is routed by them to those areas where the need for entertainment is greatest. The Commanding Officer in each theater of operations, must sanction transportation for all Camp Shows units going into his command area, and all such units are subject to his orders.

No theatrical trunk in the history of show business ever before bumped and tumbled the distances that many did for Camp Shows. As the scope of the udertaking widened, large scale musicales were added to the program of small variety units which had been the general rule in the early days. Legitimate plays, concert artists, name bands, and sports units of every kind also began to flow overseas.

The performers are not merely rehearsed, they are trained, for it takes training to prepare them for their special assignments. They do their professional jobs before the footlights, but there is more to do when the curtain comes down. As individuals as well as actors they are a link with home. Their conversations with the men are an important part of their service as are their visits to chow-lines and recreation halls, their news, their stories, their cheerfulness, the simple fact of their Americanism.

Regardless of the cost of producing them, all USO-Camp Shows are free to members of the Armed Forces. While the big stars accept no money for their services, most of the performers have been dependent on their earnings for a livelihood. They are paid salaries, more often than not considerably less than they could have earned had they stayed at home.

The end of the war brought the beginning of USO-Camp Shows' biggest job, the winning of the battle against boredom. The fall of Germany brought Camp Shows the largest order of its career. An average season on Broadway, greatest center of the commercial theater, constitutes about thirty shows, musical and dramatic. After VE-Day, Camp Shows received from the War Department a demand for 71 shows to be delivered as speedily as possible. Within ninety days Camp Shows had assembled, produced and shipped to Europe 60 new entertainment units composed of 665 entertainers—twice as many as an entire season's output on Broadway—these in addition to shows already at work in that area.

Eight of these shows were large musicales with as many as fifty people in the unit. Fifteen of them were productions of outstanding plays. Most of these had been assembled, rehearsed, costumed and tried out before soldier audiences in this country, and were awaiting shipment within six weeks of VE-Day, a performance unparalleled in the history of show business. Well within the allotted time, the entire schedule was filled and additional units were also sent to the European Theater of Operations.

The Japanese surrender brought a repetition of the demand. This time it was the largest assignment of all. Within ninety days, the Pacific Command requested that 91 units, with an estimated cast of 1,205 artists be assembled, produced and made available for that theater. In three months the work of three full Broadway seasons had to be duplicated. Camp Shows accepted the assignment.

USO-Camp Shows has been the work of many minds and many hands. Since its inception it has sent 5,424 entertainers, including stars of stage, screen and radio, to areas overseas. Show business as a whole co-operated to make this possible. Playwrights, authors and composers waived millions of dollars in royalties by permitting free usage of their properties. Producers aided in the production of their shows.

Motion picture producers made available their contract players. Executives of the entertainment business in New York and Hollywood served on voluntary talent committees that aided immeasurably in supplying Camp Shows with well-known entertainers.

No one can pay enough tribute, however, to the greatest single element contributing to the success of the Camp Shows effort: the sweat and blood of those who had to do the actual job—the actors. There can be no separate evaluation of the men and women who participated in the program. Each was great in his or her own right and all did a magnificent job as participants in the overall entertainment project. Without them and their wholehearted support, Camp Shows would not have been possible.

When they set out to bring entertainment to the troops they knew they were taking a risk. Twenty-eight of them were killed during their periods of service: when the Clipper crashed into the Tagus River at Lisbon; when airplanes crashed in France, in Alaska, and off the Italian coast; when a C-47 was reported missing somewhere near the Philippine Islands. Death came to others either before they embarked or when they were on their way to transoceanic assignments or after their arrival on foreign soil. There were some who, though still suffering from the effects of the Lisbon Clipper crash, went back to finish their job of entertaining servicemen. They knew the show must go on.

And the show will continue to go on while the need exists. Servicemen who enter the hospitals of the Veterans Administration for continued medical care will find Camp Shows still on the job bringing regular entertainment.

General Bradley, Administrator of Veterans Affairs, said upon the inception of this service at a Veterans Hospital:

"You and I are well acquainted with the work of the USO-Camp Shows overseas. We saw them in action. We know the risks and hardships that their men and women have endured so cheerfully to bring fun and relaxation to our fighting men. But a job half-done is no job at all. That's why USO-Camp Shows is here tonight. They are not leaving their job half-done. The need for their service is greater now than ever."

That USO-Camp Shows was useful to the services during the war and is needed by them still is shown by such letters as these:

From *General of the Army Dwight Eisenhower:* "Men of the Occupation Forces face the tedious task of prolonging an already long tour of duty far from their homes and friends. They will experience impatient weeks when they will appreciate, more and more, anything the folks at home can do to make their continued absence less irksome.

They will place an even higher appraisal on the smallest considerations and kindnesses—the things that bring a touch of home, the activities and events that help to brighten the routine of inaction, to occupy their time and sustain their spirit.

"Monotony and foreign surroundings combine to make their life a cheerless one. That is why . . . 'made-in-America' entertainment taken to these men by USO-Camp Shows . . . will let them know that they are not 'forgotten men.' "

From *Fleet Admiral Chester W. Nimitz:* "The American fighting men who populate the lonely and barren islands and atolls of the Pacific thoroughly appreciate the entertainment and lift to morale provided by USO-Camp Shows . . . the need for additional services of this kind will grow. I earnestly hope that the American people will continue their support."

From *General of the Army Douglas MacArthur:* "I wish to extend my personal thanks and commendation to all personnel of the USO-Camp Shows who have performed before the troops under my command.

"These men and women who have come to this theater deserve to share the pride we feel in our victory. The entertainment which they provided contributed materially to the maintenance of high morale, and it is my sincere desire that USO-Camp Shows continue its work in this theater during the occupation phase which lies ahead."

Victory Books

Over ten million books, collected in the Victory Book Campaign, were distributed to the Army and Navy, the American Merchant Marine, the American Red Cross, the War Prisoners' Aid, War Relocation Centers, and the USO.

The campaign was financed by the Red Cross and the USO, each furnishing half of the total cost of approximately $200,000. The American Library Association provided invaluable technical knowledge and leadership. The cost for each volume distributed was less than two cents.

The story of the campaign is one of whole-hearted co-operation of individuals and of groups of all kinds in communities throughout the nation. Young peoples' organizations, women's clubs, educational institutions, labor unions, churches, fraternal and patriotic orders, chambers of commerce, libraries, publishers, and business, industrial, and transportation groups aided in the collections. Retail stores used displays in their windows and placed collection boxes inside. In some cities the milkmen, the bakers, and the laundrymen collected books on their routes.

Many railroads displayed posters in their trains and installed collection boxes in their stations. Railroads granted reduced freight rates for hauling books from depot warehouses to distribution centers, and general trucking companies contributed much free long-distance transportation. The Motor Service of the Red Cross, the Salvation Army, and the American Women's Voluntary Services transported books. Schools, colleges, and universities conducted campaigns. Large corporations held drives among their employees. Advertising agencies and radio companies helped to publicize the campaign.

Folders were placed in new books urging the owner, when he had finished the book, to paste the label on the cover, tie a string around the book, affix a cent-and-a-half stamp, and send it to whichever Corps Area Headquarters was then designated as having the greatest need. Individual publishers helped also with generous donations of new books.

In one year (1943) the USO received 367,781 books for use in home operations and 43,110 were sent overseas for use in USO units in Alaska, the Panama Canal Zone, the British and Dutch Indies, Puerto Rico, Cuba, Bermuda, Newfoundland, and Brazil.

American prisoners of war in German and Italian prison camps were sometimes allowed carefully selected books. Regulations prohibited certain subjects and specified that the books must be unsoiled, contain no marks of ownership, notations, or evidence of erasure.

Emphasis was placed upon quality of books as well as quantity. Sixty per cent of the books collected were used and the basis for selection was made as strict as possible, with so many hands and minds involved in the enterprise.

Indicative of the spirit of the campaign was the phrase: "Any book you really want to keep is a good one to give."

CHAPTER VII

Outside Continental United States

(NOTE: *The USO served in certain areas outside continental United States, assigned to it by military order: Alaska, Hawaii, Canada, Newfoundland, Bermuda, Cuba, Puerto Rico, Jamaica, Trinidad, and various other Caribbean islands, the Panama Canal Zone, Brazil, other isolated spots on and opposite the coast of South America, and the Philippines.*

Overseas work in other areas—except for USO-Camp Shows—was assigned by the United States Government to the American Red Cross.

Wherever overseas the USO had clubs or mobile units many of the activities were similar to those in the States. In the following account little reference is made to standard programs common to USO's everywhere. Over the four year period, 1942 through 1945, the total attendance at overseas clubs and operations was 104,819,151 at an average cost for each man attending of nine cents.

From the extensive material available, aspects of overseas work have been chosen that indicate the general scope of the work. Frequently an activity mentioned here in connection with one place will have been carried on with equal success in another. Limitatons of space prevent a balanced description of each area. In the chapter as a whole, however, will be found many of the highlights of USO service outside the States.)

Running inland from an Alaskan port a narrow-gauge railroad, one hundred and ten miles long, penetrates some of the wildest portions of British Columbia and the Yukon. Operated by the American Army because of its importance to the Alaskan highway and the airports in the sub-Arctic, it passed through twelve wilderness stations (section houses) where soldiers, formerly employed by leading American railroads, were engaged in all kinds of operating work.

Over this narrow-gauge track once a month went one or two women from the USO in an old 1927 Paige sedan fitted with flanged wheels. At each station they left cakes, pies, books, newspapers, curtains, pictures, tobacco, and candy. From each station they collected stacks of clothing which was later distributed to the women of the port for patching, darning, mending, and buttons.

When the weather was too severe for the Paige, the USO director went by train wearing woolen shirt, moccasins in fleece-lined boots, Army issue jersey-lined slacks, pile-lined parka, and carrying her indispensable sleeping bag. The coaches had wooden seats and a stove at either end but lights were not permitted. In severe weather even the rotary plow would be held fast in the drifts between stations and to clear the tracks soldiers would work as long as thirty-six hours without a rest and with little food. Under such conditions a train leaving at nine in the morning might take until one the next morning to make the first nineteen miles.

Some of the men, isolated in these wilderness camps, became morose. The mountains in spite of their magnificent beauty bore down heavily on their spirits. Books were useful to some and one of the USO volunteers made a point of keeping such soldiers supplied. Along with extra home-cooked food, these books were sent over the railroad several times a week in the caboose of the freight train. When a soldier finished one he would send it back specifying what kind of volume he wanted next: mystery, biography, love, economics.

In other parts of Alaska the friendly residents helped the USO with fishing parties, gold-panning expeditions, dog-sled races, and all kinds of winter sports made more enjoyable for many men by ski instruction provided by USO workers. River trips including as a special feature dancing on a floating barge were scheduled in milder weather and hikes were well liked in summer. A trip to a glacier provided a real work-out when thick moss would slip from jagged rocks, the narrowness of the trail make crawling necessary, and wading ankle deep in icy water was called for when the trail followed the bed of a stream. Indispensable to the clubs were the devoted Junior Hostesses, both white and native, who met the USO's qualifications including the regulation that girls under sixteen must be accompanied by their parents or a chaperone.

Also at the fore with facilities for winter sports were USO clubs in Newfoundland. At Corner Brook servicemen had opportunities comparable to those of the finest winter resorts in this country. Salmon and trout fishing were high on the USO's list of activities as well as jigging for cod which might be immediately converted into chowder for a beach party.

At an opposite extreme were USO facilities in Bermuda featuring golf courses and bathing beaches. At one place the USO took over an elaborate hotel and an eighteen hole golf course. The surprise of GI guests was noteworthy when they found they might occupy a room, normally costing twenty dollars a day, for fifty cents or a dollar!

In Bermuda also was exemplified the extensive physical education program arranged by the Overseas Department. This varied according to the facilities available in different areas, including fully equipped gymnasiums and swimming pools. Professional instruction was available in skiing, archery, and boxing. Another special service was provided by USO workers, themselves professional physical education people, who trained GI officials for GI sports. In Bermuda an extensive sports program terminated each year in the Lily Bowl football game which the USO helped promote between the Army and Navy teams.

During the Battle of the Atlantic the USO's in Bermuda did emergency work for service personnel shipwrecked off the coast. Roaring

fires were built in club fireplaces and survivors, starving and sometimes without clothing, were cared for.

With the inclusion of 50,000 Puerto Rican troops in our military
establishment, the USO's program in the Antilles underwent drastic
change. Not only were Puerto Rican hostesses recruited in large numbers but bi-lingual staff workers became desirable, and such equipment as music and magazines was altered to fit the new need.

The problem of recruiting and training appropriate Junior Hostesses throughout the Antilles area was a challenging one. In British
Guiana girls of various racial strains co-operated in club work:
Chinese, Portuguese, East Indian, Negro, Dutch, and English. The
Georgetown club, described in one report as "the bright spot in the
colony and most certainly the only American spot," was host on two
occasions to the Governor and the prominent citizenry for broadcasts
in a "Grow More Food Campaign," thus contributing its bit toward
international good-will.

An international flavor permeated much of the area included in the
Antilles Department. The Dutch Government presented the club in
Aruba, Dutch West Indies, with a piano when the youngest princess
was born. The Canadian Army band played for USO dances in
Jamaica. In San Juan the USO conducted an all-Spanish radio pro-
gram for the benefit of Puerto Rican troops and Spanish classes were
frequently held. In Trinidad some of the Junior Hostesses were
British.

Colorful native customs and war-time conditions both had their
effect on details of club operations, whether it was the use of native
hats, five feet in diameter for club decoration, or bomber escort
provided one evening for a boatload of Junior Hostesses bound for
a dance at an isolated outpost when it became clear that only in this
way could the Navy meet the regulation that all boats in those waters
have military escort.

In the clubs themselves dances-on-order were no rarity. Thus the

Kingston USO had a standing arrangement with the Navy Intelligence Officer that when he made his first contact with the officer of an incoming ship, he might promise the men on board a dance that same night. This meant that sometimes a dance—hostesses, band, and refreshments—had to be arranged on two hours notice but when a ship appeared over the horizon everyone rose to the emergency including the club's pastry cooks who specialized in apple and lemon pies.

Both in this club and in Trinidad money changing was an important service. Military personnel, paid in American money, needed local currency when they came ashore and a club's cash turn-over might range from $300 to $500 daily. If larger requests were made at times when banks were closed, additional funds were sometimes obtained from local movie houses, secured by the USO's check.

Other Trinidad features were a regular music appreciation hour held in the parlor-lounge where no popular music was allowed, and a camera club that also used this "quiet room" for their meetings twice a month. Jewish services were held in the same place on Friday evenings.

The Port of Spain club, limited to ninety gallons of ice cream a day, found the supply never sufficient even when eked out with five or six stalks of bananas. Fifty men were often waiting in line. Here, as elsewhere, with the snack bar expanded to meet American eagerness for familiar dishes, there was a strict requirement that all employees secure a food handler's certificate before their services could be accepted. The required clean bill of health was given only by the Army medical authorities.

Equipped with sixty pairs of men's roller skates, forty pairs for women, and a cement floor, the Trinidad USO found the waiting line so long that they were forced to divide skating evenings into two periods of an hour and a half each. Recorded music was played and the skating was supervised by a floor committee of both soldiers and sailors. Among the apt pupils of American servicemen were British

Junior Hostesses. Roller skating carnivals grew to be extensive affairs
with a grand march, square dancing, and even ballet on skates.

Two leagues of twelve basketball teams each, organized in co-
operation with the Athletic and Recreation Officer, played round robin
tournaments on Sundays and Mondays. During the course of an
afternoon's or an evening's play as many as eight hundred men might
be spectators.

The USO's work at overseas bases was often complicated by differing social customs. That any country through such an organization as
the USO should spend money and effort for the comfort and pleasure
of enlisted personnel, was so surprising to residents of some areas as
to be difficult of comprehension. In places having such an attitude,
the USO had some difficulty acquiring buildings for clubs in respectable areas of the city.

The story of how the USO secured and held a respected status in
its work overseas was one of patience, adroitness, and undeviating
adherence to standards accepted as a matter of course within continental United States. In the single matter of Junior Hostesses a considerable span of time was often involved between plans and their
execution. In some places girls of the type the USO meant to have in
the clubs were not allowed to join in the activities until the father of
the family had been formally waited upon by an official representative
of the USO, and he and his family invited to visit the club. Then if
arrangements there impressed him favorably he might, in due course,
permit his daughters to attend—duly chaperoned.

But in overseas bases, no more than in continental United States,
was the mere presence of girls considered sufficient. Certain standard
practices were part of accepted USO procedure. Girls were invited to
the clubs not to amuse themselves but for the entertainment of the
servicemen. This meant they must learn to do certain things in the
accepted American way and for many, USO training meant an extended social horizon. It served also in some instances as a revelation

of new possibilities of individual development for young women whose sheltered upbringing had been a limiting experience. For other civilian residents of some of the areas where the USO had clubs the total operation represented the first demonstration they had seen of a democratic institution in action.

Occasionally a USO was the means by which servicemen came in contact with a side of life in a foreign city they would otherwise have missed. Such was the case when a USO in Brazil arranged to have a well-known singer of aristocratic family give a concert in the club. Aside from a glamorous appearance, she was a woman of great personal charm and a large audience received her with enthusiasm. Afterward when she passed through the main part of the club on the way to her car, she was greeted with applause from every corner; and when she reached the large entrance lobby every man in it rose to his feet—a spontaneous gesture of respect that not only impressed the singer but all the other Brazilians who were present.

USO clubs spotted along the hump of Brazil's coastline spanned such distances that the local supervisor found it necessary to fly some 100,000 miles a year. The men these units served were carefully not mentioned in newspaper headlines those days: men involved in the anti-submarine patrol; men stationed at the headquarters of the South Atlantic Fleet and crews from those ships; men at airbases including one of the largest in the world that played a vital part in the North African campaign and later serviced B-29s.

Live entertainment bulked large in the USO's morale-sustaining program in the majority of overseas clubs. In one year alone (1945) the total attendance at live shows produced by the Overseas Department was 6,716,983. Among these were the shows that the Navy flew from Rio every few weeks for the entertainment of service personnel scattered up and down the coast and stationed on adjacent islands.

In the Panama Canal Zone were featured informal educational programs—classes and discussion groups—that were included in the

38,376,423 group activities in overseas operations during the period, January 1942 to the close of 1945. As in continental United States all sorts of topics were covered. In the Canal Zone classes in Spanish were a major interest. One of them in which nearly a hundred men were enrolled—taught by a Panamanian woman of Spanish descent married to an American—used a conversational approach with emphasis on the history, traditions, and current worthwhile attractions of Panama. Another program development that proved to be of exceptional interest, both to service personnel and to newly arrived defense workers, was a series of Panama Book and Author talks, sponsored by the USO's library committee.

In both the Canal Zone and Hawaii much of the USO's success was due to groups of American women who had organized for service to military personnel before USO's were established. Generously and capably co-operative, they affiliated with the USO in due course and were responsible for some of its finest achievements.

Mobile service out of the Canal Zone was important to many isolated units—searchlight, weather, radar, barrage balloon. Sometimes there would be as few as twenty or twenty-five men in jungle clearings accessible only by two-seater planes or by boat. On one island to which the USO took a live show and extra girls for a dance, chemical warfare research was being carried on. This was a boat trip of three and a half hours each way.

For many isolated bases dramatic entertainment had its uses. Sometimes professional or amateur talent could be flown in or brought by boat. In other places where the number of men was large enough, they were encouraged by USO specialists in dramatics to put on their own shows. In advance of this specialist's arrival the men might arrange several unrelated acts. These might be recast into a longer, integrated show when she appeared, equipped with the latest hit-parade sheet music, a complete make-up kit, sketches written by top revue writers, gag books, diagrams for all kinds of stage lighting and production equipment.

In connection with troop transports going through the Panama Canal the USO's in the Zone had a special assignment. Often these men were not permitted off their ships and in such cases the USO sometimes took the dramatic entertainment which they had arranged locally, with either professional or amateur talent, onto ships including battleships and carriers both at anchor and at dock.

On the carriers the elevator could be raised for use as a stage for men watching the show from the flight deck. At other times the USO performances were given on the pier itself while the men sat on the ship's guns and crowded every vantage point. Now and then the men would volunteer talent of their own to prolong the show and a sailor-accordionist might play familiar songs far into the moonlit night, the volume of men's voices drowning the few sopranos of the entertainment troop.

Again service personnel on transports might be allowed on shore on the one condition that they join a USO sight-seeing tour. The USO, foreseeing some such development, had previously conducted a training course for volunteers willing to serve as guides. The heaviest single day involved seven hundred men in one group. For such a mob as this the twenty available Army and Navy buses were not sufficient and eight trucks were pressed into service. A sound truck was then ordered in between the first four and the last four with a guide who proceeded to broadcast to all of them at once—and incidentally to the general countryside.

Another service which the overseas USO's performed was shopping for enlisted personnel. For some of the Canal Zone clubs, filling orders sent back to them by men who had gone on into forward areas was a major responsibility. The detail of the orders, the patience and ingenuity of the shoppers were impressive. One urgent GI who had not been in funds at the time of his shore leave in a Canal Zone city, sent a map of the central part of town along with his order. He explained that if the director would walk according to the arrow past such and such a fountain, diagonally across a park, take a certain right hand turn and then go to the left, he would come to a little shop the name of which the boy did not remember but there in the window he would see an alligator bag whose price he did not know (he thought it was around fifty dollars) but the director would be able to identify the bag easily because it had a baby alligator mounted on it! And of course the director did find it, sent it to the little woman in the States, advised the GI that he had done so, and returned the change.

It was not, however, until the redeployment period following the end of the war in Europe that the Canal Zone's service to troop transports developed its most unique feature. In those days high-point men, too essential to be discharged, were being taken straight to the Pacific war without any leave in the States. For military reasons, they would not be allowed off their ships in the Canal Zone.

A Commanding Officer in the Canal Zone who knew what a few hours on land would mean to these men, ordered a barricade constructed at one pier area that included, with some two acres of land, a USO club.

Within twenty-four hours the barricade was up, and the Army moved in to construct Red Cross shacks, a PX, and long wooden benches. Within these two acres, during this period, was demonstrated one of the best examples of complete co-operation between the Military, the Red Cross, the civilian community, and the USO. The redeployment men putting in at this point were given complete freedom of this restricted area. Coming off the piers they could stop for information about friends or relatives in the Canal Zone, receive ice cream, buy all kinds of essentials, or wander to the USO club where on an indoor stage almost continuous entertainment was furnished. The military authorities also permitted letter writing in the club. Catholic, Protestant, and Jewish chaplains were present in case any of the men desired their services.

In this special pier area a shopping service was installed. Men wishing to make purchases were given an envelope on the front of which were listed articles available in the town with their prices. Any item desired was checked, the money for it sealed into the envelope, and the order handed out to the shopping committee waiting outside the barricade limits.

Hot dogs, rolls, and coffee were served at this pier-area USO by many civilian volunteers and the story goes that supplying the rolls was a major problem with the club's first order amounting to 14,000. Such a number, the local bakeries were utterly unable to furnish. The Army came to the rescue and helped bake but even its machines were unable to keep up with the demand. A call went out for more bakers and GIs from the ranks fell to shaping dough by hand with the result that the USO snack bar met the needs of its hungry clientele.

Usually these troop transports, carrying from three to six thousand men, stopped for no more than a twenty-four hour period but once, at the beginning of the pier-area service, a ship was detained for four days while repairs were made. Determined to uphold its standard of new entertainment on each occasion, the USO put on four different shows those four successive nights.

For numbers of men served, Hawaii held a record of its own with seventy-six clubs and units, setting an all-time high in one month of two and a quarter million men in attendance.

But quantity was by no means the only standard in that Territory. Problems of such volume, involving the usual direct services of the USO, demanded a high degree of resourceful administration. Mass activities were of necessity at the fore: dancing, dramatic entertainment, sight-seeing trips. Of this last the Hawaiian clubs made a specialty in the belief that seeing the Islands was not only interesting in itself but valuable in helping men to feel more at home in this area which served at one time or another as the home base for most men in the Pacific.

Here they had their final training before such campaigns as Tarawa, the Gilberts, the Marshalls, the Marianas, Iwo Jima, and the Philippines. It was from here they left for combat duty, knowing that the next time they saw ground over the bow of their landing barges, it would be a beachhead. And it was Hawaii that welcomed them back, still wearing their camouflaged uniforms from Saipan and Iwo Jima for rest, retraining, and reconditioning. Here was a morale problem, complicated, varied, great in extent, of long continued urgency.

Running excerpts from an annual Hawaiian report show some of the ways in which this urgent need has been met by one or more of the USO operations in the Territory:

"Through a series of community days, the average GI learned more in a few hours about the lore and color of these islands than he could ever hope to learn in months of aimless knocking about . . . for the community people who staged these days for him brought to them the old and the genuine and the cherished." The first was the Chinese Day put on by Chinese Americans. The Japanese, Korean, and Hawaiian communities presented similar days, "and GI horizons were heightened, and their appreciation of the scope of that for which they fight enlarged when the Japanese Americans worked for weeks to make their day an unforgettable one at the club. All the women who participated were mothers of Americans of Japanese ancestry then fighting in Italy."

The program philosophy of one club refused "to accept the idea that when a fellow doffs civvies he also loses his mental and cultural curiosity . . . So while a comedian tossed pies in the theater for the men who wanted a laugh more than anything in the world, the adjacent lounge was hung with some of the finest art in the possession of the Honolulu Academy of Art for the men who knew another type of hunger. And the roof garden that normally shrieked with swing for the jitterbugs was quiet one night a week as men worked at their easels capturing the new charm of an Oriental model."

"During 1944, GIs of the Jewish faith were helped both in their religious and individual needs by area workers on Oahu and Hawaii. Regular visits were made to wounded men in hospitals and letters sent to their parents. . . . Religious services were scheduled weekly, and transportation arranged for boys at outlying posts. . . . In April, Passover Seders were held at posts throughout Oahu and at Kamuela and Haili Street USO's on Hawaii. On this island alone 5,000 men participated in the observance of this religious festival."

At a time when war workers in Honolulu were estimated at 100,-000, the USO lent something of a hand in helping workers find living quarters. By the early fall of 1944 "it was taking to workers in the Pearl Harbor and Naval Housing area a total of eighteen different classes, in addition to tours, picnics, and parties. Another innovation was the summer program for war workers' children. . . ."

A nurse, the USO has found, "doesn't want any fanfare. But after, say, a 36-hour flight from Saipan in an evacuation plane (with no doctor aboard and the welfare of twenty patients her complete responsibility), she could sure go for a hot bath and a long stretch on the beach, with the wind to dispel the smell of medications and the sun to smooth the kinks out of her body." For nurses a USO beach cottage was available. "As one put it facetiously—but with an undertone in her voice—'This is where I come to get my brave new face back on straight again.' "

Negroes coming into the Territory "put on one of the most successful programs ever staged in Hawaii—the Pacific Jubilee which was produced by fourteen Negro military units and attended by 28,339 guests at the USO Victory Club. This day-long program featured outstanding bands, crafts, and entertainment. The hit of the program was the drill on Bethel Street by a crack platoon of Negro Marines. . . ."

Oahu's dance groups were called the Flying Squadron and the Hui Menehune, Junior Hostesses who volunteered as partners for dances on the posts. Waiting to be transported by trucks, buses, or command cars, "they look as though they've just stepped out of a bandbox instead of high school or the office. The majority of them have been attending enlisted men's dances for three years. Some of them have never missed one, and they average three or four a week. These youngsters, the greatest morale builders in existence, take great pride in their organization. There's only one rule they occasionally break. They have been known to chew gum on the dance floor. But USO never seems to notice. They know all the girls accept gum because it's all the boys have to offer them, and they want so much to give them something in return."

Nearly half a million isolated GIs were visited by the mobile canteen in one year and well ahead of time thousands of red, green, and white tarlatan Christmas stockings were made and filled with gifts donated by many organizations. "Mobile canteens, private vehicles, GI command cars and trucks were pressed into service for the celebration. Decorated with fireplaces, tiny Christmas trees, wreaths, Nativity scenes and winter displays, the fleet made its way to outposts all over Oahu. . . . A few nights later a GI reported: 'Gee, we were just like a bunch of kids after you left! We all sat down and dug into our socks, sang every carol on the sheet, then I emptied mine, folded up the sock, put it in an envelope, and sent it home to my own kid.'"

"Laughter echoed from the throats of 2,142,830 GIs in 1944. It rang from hundreds of theaters that had stars for a roof, and mud or dust for seats. From the decks of aircraft carriers, from troopships in Pearl Harbor before weighing anchor for the battlefronts, from hospital wards where the battlefronts had returned their maimed and shocked. It was shouted from island to island in the Territory as the shows toured the 'pineapple circuit,' and for three unforgettable days it shattered the quiet of the island of Midway, when a USO unit was flown to that bitterly fought-for atoll . . . the first women to set foot on it since December 7, 1941. The girls were mobbed, and men cheered themselves hoarse at this reminder that, at that dimly recalled place known as home, there were women like this, waiting for them.

"Of all the remembered laughter of a year, that of a round-faced, clear-eyed kid comes back most vividly when this observer shared his poncho on the rocky ground for an outdoor performance of the USO Theatrical Division's show, '4.0'. It surged up, seemingly, from the very toes of his clumsy boots. It bubbled over and spilled on everyone around it, lighting their faces. He threw back his head and shouted it to the sky. Caught in the gales of his own laughter he rocked helplessly, clutching his aching sides, the tears rolling down his cheeks. When the two USO comedians wound up their act and disappeared from the stage, it wasn't a moment too soon; the kid was about to bust.

"When he had subsided to an occasional ripple, he lay back limply on the ground, closed his eyes, and with a great sigh of content, said to the world in general, '*Man,* it's wonderful to laugh!'"

With the liberation of the Philippines came one further overseas assignment for the USO. And this time the responsibility for opening clubs had to be shouldered regardless of the fact that there were neither buildings nor supplies, but simply the need for them. As rapidly as possible several bomb-shattered structures were patched up in Manila, in the Batangas area, at Taal Beach, and at Angeles—all on Luzon. Materials were shipped from the States and from Hawaii. USO personnel was flown in. Ten clubs were opened within a matter of weeks after General MacArthur's authorization though a number lacked windows or doors and all were short of equipment, measured by accepted club standards in the States.

To recreation-hungry GIs, they were USO's, however, with hamburgers, ice cream, movies, and parties. Where transportation and manpower shortages temporarily caused the USO to offer less than its usual service the United States Army helped all it could and GIs individually were more than ready to take the will for the full deed and quickly volunteered to help with the reconstruction.

That this early, somewhat handicapped service had value is indicated by a report written in the summer of 1945, describing general conditions: "All the experiences of bewilderment, unfamiliarity, discomfort, helplessness descended upon the individual entering Manila. It's not the strangeness of a foreign place because in such a place you feel order, different though it may be from your previous experiences, and you can sense security, comforted in knowing that, if others have it, there is a way for you to obtain it.

"But in Manila you are immediately aware of a tremendous disruption, a shattering of all that creates balance. . . . The stench of decay—animal and vegetable—rides the overpowering dust into the very bottom of your lungs and under your collar and cuffs. Then it issues in moist waves from the mud of a moment later, gagging you.

"The incredible destruction and the litter of war that seems to cover the open spaces that held nothing to be destroyed depresses you so that you wonder why everyone and everything doesn't go somewhere else and start over again. . . . The shocking examples of force that crumbled earthquake-proof walls and ripped shreds of concrete from massive columns to leave them hanging in mid-air from strands of steel. . . .

"The utter lack of the small conveniences and little luxuries you once took for granted brings childish happiness when you find one—not in Manila, though, for there is none, but in that sort of floating world within Manila that is the Army installation. You boast of having a cold drink, acquiring a sheet or pillow, having seen yourself in a mirror, getting a shower instead of a bucket bath or finding a flush toilet—that works. . . .

"The pounding, grinding, crashing noises of unceasing military activity that sweeps everything before it drives you into yourself so that every nerve in your body tries to hold you from entering the torrential flow of men and machines along the streets and sidewalks. You develop a reverence for the thought of quietness, comfort, and the state of being clean.

"Small wonder then that merely to walk through a doorway marked 'USO' releases from your subconscious much of the pressure it bears and affords an escape into a pleasantly familiar atmosphere. . . . Small wonder, either, that you very often fail to get beyond the nearest chair during the first fifteen minutes past that doorway!"

Hello, USO! was a common greeting from men on the march in the early weeks of Philippine liberation. When traffic was halted, they would call across to USO jeeps or accost USO uniforms with questions as to where the clubs were located. "We'd like to try some of your home-made food!" they would shout.

Into the clubs they swarmed, nearly two million in attendance during the last six months of 1945. Somehow the short-handed directors kept the places going, planning programs with as much variety as possible while they rushed building repairs, hired employees, secured needed materials from anywhere and everywhere. (Vari-colored parachutes and dyed burlap were found to make good drapes for club interiors.) Meanwhile party refreshments were dished up in USO kitchens on field stoves. Bulletin boards, constructed from salvage material, displayed maps of the islands as well as lists of available recreation features.

Program plans included all the usual USO activities that facilities made possible. Roller skating ranked high in popularity as did dances and all forms of dramatic entertainment. Music gained and held headline status—group singing, chamber music, symphony orchestras, native songs in costume. Crafts, especially work in leather, were well received. Sports of all sorts, indoor and out, were enthusiastically patronized as rapidly as opportunity permitted.

Requests for personal services were frequent, especially from men getting ready to leave: questions on discharge, employment, home adjustments. Forums were held on job opportunities for servicemen. Tours to The Walled City attracted those with historical interest in their new location.

At snack bars with American food, ice cream probably topped the list of favorites. To be sure of a cup, men would line up before it was frozen. And when no spoons were to be had, "sipping" ice cream became accepted practice.

Nor were food activities confined to club buildings. With USO

assistance Junior Volunteers and GIs might jointly plan a picnic:
"Packed into GI trucks, well supplied with GI, volunteer, and USO
food, the group left the USO about 10 a.m. and journeyed to Los
Banos some forty kilometers away. There lunch was spread and the
participants ate and danced, ate and swam, ate and played baseball!"
Trips to other lakes, to beaches and mountains were frequent.

One club discovered that the post office had thousands of magazines
and books it could not deliver because the addressees could not be
reached. Many of these were turned over to the USO which distributed them to isolated troops and to hospitals.

As club programs have developed the volunteers in the Philippines
have grown in numbers and in variety of services rendered—both the
Junior and Senior Volunteers. Some of them have said that giving
co-operation to the USO is one way they can repay their 'liberators.'
Living conditions, however, pose serious difficulties to any sort of
civilian organization. According to one staff report from the area:
"Few streets have signs and many are a series of holes joined by
dust. . . . The Manila people live in lean-to's, dug-outs, settlement
houses, and in all kinds of homes far from their pre-war addresses so
that none knows where anyone else lives. We strive to understand
how a group of volunteers ever appear for a program. . . ."

Another function of the USO in the Philippines is serving as a
clearing-house for servicemen from the same state or town. "The
Stateside Hometown Registers are thumb-printed and finger-marked
where the boys have tried to locate someone from their own towns,"
comes word from Manila. "One register, four hours after it opened,
had 750 registrants with every state in the Union represented. There
is great excitement when men from the same town or state get together. Maybe they were in high school together, maybe they be-
longed to the same scout troop. Maybe they were merely acquaintances, but they are all buddies here. The old home town, the village
green, the high school, the corner drug store with its sundae specials,

all these bring back the days-when, and the boys enjoy a tremendous relief from this bombed city with its teeming population of saddened, starved people. The American serviceman who has had a tour of overseas duty is returning home with a new appreciation of his home life, be it in the smallest village or the largest city."

And for Our Allies

(NOTE: *The few excerpts from club reports quoted below may give some indication of the way USO's tried to serve members of the armed forces of our Allies, temporarily in this country. That clubs were often able to provide hosts and hostesses who spoke the language of their guests—no matter which Allied nation they might have come from—emphasized the "nation-of-nations" quality of the country and the value of a common channel for achieving a common purpose.*)

From a Major came the wire: "Train of RAAF will arrive this p.m. Can you have 150 girls meet train to make acquaintance. Will stop 45 minutes." A gasp of astonishment but "when the train pulled in a right respectable number were on hand to meet the Australian boys. The Aussies, who had been in this country only three days, were obviously impressed."

On the Canadian border "the first USO club in America has opened for the exclusive use of all servicewomen of the United Nations."

"When over one hundred Russians appeared on an 'off' night, only two or three of whom spoke English, an emergency call brought in fifty Junior Hostesses and soon polka steps and jitterbug rhythm became the language of the group."

"A British servicewoman was having a spot of tea in our USO while she listened to symphonic recordings."

"For the Chinese cadets in this area we had open house: Mah Jong, card games, and a Chinese lesson for the American hostesses. At the end of the evening everyone danced."

"The women's auxiliary of the Polish War Veterans were hostesses to the boys of our club recently. A buffet lunch of Polish meats, breads, and punch was served and the Polish Rhythm Orchestra furnished the music."

"When Royal Air Force men appear at the club, the hostess sets a pot of water on to boil so they can make English tea in their own special way."

"Frequent visitors are three soldiers from the European battle-ground of Poland, Hungary, and Czecho-Slovakia. The club's home hospitality committee has located neighborhood families whose members speak the language of the men and entertain them."

"Honing their razors in the washroom of our club this morning were: a young Polish soldier whose family is confined in a German concentration camp; a young Englishman who lost two brothers in RAF battles; a Frenchman grieving over a young wife missing in occupied France; and an Athenian who was notified by the Red Cross last month that his father had died of starvation in Greece and that his only brother is classed as 'missing.'"

"Most of the French training near here have seen much active service; many of them have lost families and homes within the last few years, and some have escaped from German prison camps. Consequently they are a pretty sober group of young men. At one USO party given for them an American officer remarked with relief that it was the first time he had ever known a certain young Frenchman, with a row of decorations on his chest, to smile or laugh."

CHAPTER VIII

Migration to Industry

The late afternoon sun lay warm on the trailer camp. Mrs. Kroger had let down the side step of her trailer and was sitting on it. She was waiting for a man who wanted to talk to her. Miss Delancy, the USO lady, had told her he would come around five o'clock.

It was good to sit, sun or no sun, after eight hours of standing on your feet. At first it had been her arms that gave her trouble, shoving heavy projectiles around. But now it was her feet.

She had changed out of her regulation work clothes—a dull tan coverall with a cap so her hair couldn't come loose and catch in the power machinery—and in honor of the man coming, had put on a freshly washed gingham. Real gingham, too, she said to herself with pleasure, smoothing the blue, green, and white plaid on her knee and admiring the sheerness of the fine weave—nothing like this sleazy wartime stuff.

The camp was reasonably quiet. The swing shift had gone on and the graveyard folks including her eighteen year old daughter, Helen, weren't real wide awake yet. The unusual stillness was pleasant to Mrs. Kroger. While she didn't care for a place with no life at all, she could do forever without that part of the usual racket that was bickering—or worse—between neighbors. A neighbor, she was thinking, meant something different here from what it had where she'd come from. At home neighbors were your friends who lived nearby. Here your neighbors were the folks whose trailer was up against yours. A certain amount of arguing was usually going on. There were some fights too, of course. It was a strain for everybody to be uprooted like all these folks were here. People missed not having anything they were used to.

From the little knoll on which their trailer stood, Mrs. Field could get a good view of the whole camp—about 500 trailers now and 36 states represented, the last time she and her sixteen year old son, Burt, had checked up on the licenses.

Straight across the way was the USO trailer. Mrs. Kroger took considerable secret pride in being its neighbor. She and Miss Delancy had hit it off from the first day when the newcomer had come over to get her advice about some housekeeping matters.

Her daughter, Helen, had liked the USO woman too ever since that first evening when she'd asked Helen if she and her friends on the graveyard shift had organized a Dawn Patrol Club yet. They hadn't but Helen had been crazy to get one going when Miss Delancy got through telling her how much fun they were.

She'd been proud of her daughter that night—she'd spoken up so pert and told the USO newcomer just what things were like. "Everything is hurry, hurry, hurry at the Plant," she'd told her. "When you get through you're too keyed up to go to bed. But at eight o'clock in the morning, what's there to do?"

"There could be picnic breakfasts outdoors," Miss Delancy had told her. "And early morning bicycle trips, and maybe we can rig up a roller skating rink. Once they get the USO clubhouse built there'll be movies that time of day, of course."

"But I'm luckier than lots of the girls," Helen had gone on. "I've got a trailer to go home to. The girls who come in on buses—especially the swingshift crowd—they have an awful time."

"Getting through at midnight, you mean?"

"Yeah and no buses back out into the country where they live until

seven o'clock in the morning. There isn't even a movie open where
they can go and sleep. Some of them lie down on the station benches
but there isn't room enough for everybody. And then there are all
those boys—"

"What boys?"

Mrs. Kroger told her because she'd talked to a cop about those boys.
He'd said it beat him how you could tell whether all the boys on
street corners at night were loitering or waiting for buses. If the Plant
didn't change the shifts so often maybe he could get to know the boys.
But like it was he never knew where he was at.

"Of course the few girls who can get rooms in town don't have it
so bad," Helen had explained to Miss Delancy. "I know four who
share one room—but boy, do they pay a price and no laundry privileges either! They work different shifts so they can take turns in the
two beds."

Mrs. Kroger knew that overcrowding still went on. Miss Delancy
seemed to think something could be done about it when the new
housing project opened up. From her seat on the trailer steps Mrs.
Kroger looked across the little creek to the rising ground some distance beyond where these new buildings cluttered up the view—row
after row of little houses all alike. She had heard a rumor that the
trailerites who'd been there longest were to have first chance at any
vacancies in the housing project after the latest batch of essential-
war-workers had been taken care of. She wouldn't live in one of those
houses just like everybody else's for anything. They looked as though
they had been cut with the same cookie cutter and as Mrs. Kroger
contemplated the possibility of living in one of them she felt the sharp,
constricting imprint of a pattern coming down on her.

Just the same she took a certain pride in being sure they would be
offered to her if to anybody on the basis of long residence. There had
been only three trailers standing in the field the day the Plant manager
had pointed it out to her and told her to pick her parking lot.

Things had changed since those early days. For awhile—before central incinerators were put in—folks just buried their garbage over near the swamp. One spring, down in the low part of the field, had done for all of them. There'd been nothing but outdoor privies—a couple in the edge of the woods. But when the management began digging pits for a dozen more up on the hillside Mrs. Kroger got several women to go with her to protest. They talked nicely to the manager because they thought maybe he didn't know, as all farm women did, that you mustn't ever have your outhouses on higher ground than your drinking water for fear seepage might start a typhoid epidemic.

The manager had been right decent and pretty soon a cement building had been put up in a good location. Flush toilets were installed and in a separate room at one end four washing machines with meters so that for a dime or a quarter you could do quite a bunch of laundry.

This laundry had been the only place they'd had to welcome Miss Delancy when she'd made her first trip here without her trailer. That afternoon seemed a long time ago though it was only a few months back. Miss Delancy sure was a fast worker but she said the jobs needing to be done piled up faster still. She seemed to worry most of all because the young folks had no place to have a good time together. Every place near the Plant there was cat-calling night and day and lots of the girls with time on their hands couldn't resist a cat-call whether they knew the boy or not. But where could couples go to have a little harmless fun?

"They've got a right to be hilarious," Miss Delancy said. "But we've got to provide them with the right sort of place." As soon as the USO club was opened they'd have a dance every Saturday, she said, running all the time no matter when you came off your shift.

The shadows were getting longer now and off to the right, less than a mile away, the tall smoke-stacks and the angular bulk of the Plant where they all worked took on a blue-gray tinge. But it wasn't necessary to see the smoke-stacks to know they were there, Mrs. Kroger thought grimly. The soot saw to that—settling down on everything from the white morning glories she had so carefully trained up the twine trellis below the side window to the white crocheted mat on top of the radio just inside the sill.

Even without the smoke there would have been plenty of dust to keep a housekeeper constantly on the job. So few of the trailer people would bother with little lawns around their trailers even though the manager would furnish water and a hose for sprinkling. She and Burt, working quietly outside while Helen slept inside the trailer, had had a patch of grass and a border of zinnias even when they had to carry the water in pails from the creek. In her opinion there wasn't much use living if you didn't have some grass and flowers. Recently they had had to make a low fence out of irregular splints from orange crates to keep the raft of new children from trampling down the flowers. It spoiled the looks of the place a little, but in such close quarters you had to manage as you could.

Across the roadway she watched a beagle hound and a child of about equal length stretched out in the dirt playing lazily with a section of old tire. She doubted if the child had had a bath in the six months since its family had moved here. When Mrs. Kroger went shopping in the nearest town and heard people talking about "trailer trash," it was this child's family she thought of. Of course there were too many of them for one trailer but she felt sure they were the kind of people who, even in a nice clean country kitchen, would dirty the place up.

She thought of her own country kitchen, of the gold star she had left hanging in the window because it somehow made leaving home less hard if some token of her man, Ed, stayed behind to hold the old way together even if it could never be the same again.

She still felt they had done right to close the house, buy the trailer, and come. At least she had been sure until just lately when Burt, who was so big for sixteen, had taken up with a new crowd that had a car. Right now he was off with them again. Until recently she hadn't worried about Burt too much. Before Ed joined up he had told her they must remember the boy was almost grown now; they must let him make some decisions for himself. But the first one he had made after his father's death—that he would get into the service as soon as he possibly could—she had done her best to change. She could understand how he felt about wanting to take his father's place. But she had tried to make him understand that even his father's outfit, the Seabees, had had to have what the factories made. She had been so thankful when he had agreed to come along with her to the Plant.

They were snug in the trailer, up on blocks with its precious tires stored safely under the bunks. Still Burt had said several times lately he got tired of nothing to do evenings but listen to the radio squawking. A worried look came into Mrs. Kroger's face. She had selected the Plant rather than one much nearer their home, because this one was in the country instead of bordering a city. A city, she still felt, would have put too many bad things in a boy's way. But when some of these young fellows she didn't know anything about drove up the narrow way between the trailers in an old car minus fenders, but covered with pictures and signs daubed on with yellow paint, Mrs. Kroger didn't feel so sure about the place. There were honkey-tonks and worse spots not far down the road and she knew it was easy for a kid to follow a crowd—especially when he was tired of doing the same thing over and over in a factory and had no place else to go for fun.

"Pardon me," a pleasant-looking man suddenly appeared around the corner and took off his hat with a stiff sort of courtesy, enough like her own man's to make her swallow. "Pardon me, but I'm looking for a Mrs. Kroger."

"You've found her. Sit down." She had carried out to the little patch of grass one of their two straight chairs.

"My name is Wilson." He sat down, his hat across his knees. He seemed just friendly enough but not a know-it-all.

"Miss Delancy told me she thought perhaps you and your son—
Burt's his name, isn't it?—would be interested in having a ball team
started—"

When Mr. Wilson drove back to his room that night he wasn't
sure whether Mrs. Kroger was sold to his plan or not. She had told
him very plainly what the situation was like for boys. She didn't seem
sure that much could be done about it.

At first he felt provoked by her lack of response. He had counted
on her—not only to fall in with his plan, but to be enthusiastic. These
trailer camps were the toughest assignment he had had in years of
community welfare work. What made it so hard was that you were
not generally wanted in this situation. The townpeople—"the na-
tives"—were apt to cold-shoulder you because many of them didn't
want the trailer people to be better satisfied than they were. They
thought the newcomers were a nuisance and would be glad if they
hated it enough here to go back where they came from.

On the other hand most of the newcomers had been so snubbed by
the old residents that they now distrusted the motives of anyone who
tried to make things more pleasant for them. They weren't inclined
to take chances on new-fangled notions. If conditions got too bad
they'd rather just move on. The drag of such labor turnover on war
production did not come alive for them in personal terms.

He knew that work in over-burdened war production communities
had been included in the USO's earliest plans. Well did he remember
the sternly emphatic words of a high Government official talking
about meeting the leisure-time needs of industrial workers: "Not so
glamorous as entertaining the young men in our armed forces but
certainly of equal importance. . . . Without relaxation and change,
morale, productive activity and health are threatened—and that is
something national defense cannot afford." Helping to keep up the
morale of industrial war workers was the USO's contribution to production. A man couldn't put everything he had into his job if he was

worried sick. And in these days of transplanted families, all kinds of worries could distract a man. The USO tried to relieve some of this strain through a variety of activities that included services for his wife and children as well as for himself.

Next day Mr. Wilson got permission from the manager of the trailer court to block off one of the streets between the trailers, hang a screen at one end and show a movie. Long before dark the children began to drag blankets out of the trailers to sit on, often with a puppy tugging at one corner, and a number of chairs for older people were stationed at vantage points. Mr. Wilson decided to run two pictures with a little intermission between. This pause would give him a chance to talk to the fathers and mothers around the fringe of the audience and get their reaction to setting up a ball team.

While he waited for it to get dark he hunted up the manager, a rather heavy-set fellow who seemed inclined to be friendly though there were always worried lines between his eyes. Mr. Wilson offered him a cigar, lit one himself, and listened to quite a spiel about the youngsters who didn't have anything to do Sunday mornings.

"Saturdays are bad enough. But most every trailer has something going on on Saturdays—marketing or washing up for Sunday or getting some cooking done ahead. So the kids feel in on the busyness. But Sundays the old man sleeps or their ma wants to sit down a minute peaceful and the kids is just—on the court, as you might say. Or another way of puttin' it is, that they're on *me*."

"What kind of mischief do they get into?"

"Fights of course, all the time fights. But I don't pay them much mind unless somebody gets really messed up and then mostly their mas take over. But lately they been stripping the lemon trees along the south side of the court property and using 'em for hand grenades. The fella who owns that orchard wasn't too keen on renting me this space. If he finds his crop is being ruint over on this side, he's likely not to renew."

"Didn't I see an old trolley car parked on the far edge of your lot?"

The manager nodded vigorously. "I had that hauled up here think-ing it'd give the kids something to do but the newness soon wore off."

"It'd make a place to have small meetings, though."

"Sure would. I been fixin' to get a Sunday School held there if I could just find a woman to do the teachin'. And," he added less hope-fully, "chairs for the little brats to sit on."

"Hey, mister," a small boy interrupted, "when you goin' to get goin'? It's blacker'n a black cat outside now."

Mr. Wilson emerged immediately into the twilight and asked his young companion if he'd help him carry the films. "Don't you think a gray cat would be nearer the truth, son?"

There was quite a big turn-out and Mr. Wilson decided to show his best film first. This was a good projector and he didn't have to pay much attention to it so while the film ran off he fell to thinking about other tough spots in the country he knew about where small towns or rural areas had been suddenly turned into large centers of industry and the USO had lent a hand. One place had been nothing but sagebrush and buckthorn a few years back. Then on the bottom of a dry lake some 8,000 people had moved in to do a war work job. This eight thousand had included many families, some hundred and fifty Army personnel, several hundred war prisoners, and 1,500 Negro troops. The USO had certainly had all it could handle in that place!

It was especially tough going, Mr. Wilson felt, when your organiza-tion hadn't any headquarters nearby where you could make new-comers feel welcome. If they did have, it would be so easy to say, "Come on over and use the swimming pool" or "We've got some bowling and boxing contests on tonight. You might like to try out for them" or again "How about joining one of our classes in practical mechanics? It might serve as a refresher course or maybe help you to a promotion in your job." Of course some of these things could be managed, once the Government got the recreation building here ready for the USO to operate.

Another spot he had in mind hadn't been anything but a railroad station with about forty people living within a mile of it. He'd heard lately that there were now 5,000 housing units and apartments for civilians there and barracks for twelve to fifteen thousand enlisted men. Over and over the story could be repeated: small communities suddenly mushrooming as industry located nearby—powder plants, ship building, supply depots and repair bases, ordnance plants, plants at work on aspects of the atomic bomb.

By the following Saturday morning, Mr. Wilson had the nucleus of two good rival ball teams with Burt Kroger showing promise as a pitcher. Most of the youngsters in the trailer camp and housing projects, too young to play, came to watch and umpire. Nothing like competition for bringing out the crowd. Fathers also dropped by to watch before turning into bed or going on to work. Mr. Wilson talked to these men about setting up a committee or two among the trailer and housing project people. Wouldn't they like to have some little organization so they could take over themselves such matters as recreation for the youngsters, maybe Saturday night dances, or even group picnics?

As Mr. Wilson watched these people from almost every state in the union, he saw them begin to realize that any group this size ought to have its own democratically chosen committee to look after its common interests. There were elements of the old New England town meeting in all this. Managing their own public affairs would go a long way to make these men, transplanted from their homes, feel secure in their new life. The quicker they could take over the responsibility for making out of this new community something more stable than a mere collection of individual trailers or of buildings in a housing project, the more settled they would feel.

"I got sixty chairs," said the trailer manager unexpectedly one day. "Now if I could get a teacher, I'd have a Sunday School going in that old trolley car. Got any suggestions about how I could go about the teacher end?"

"I've got a hunch or two. Let me see what I can do. I'll get in touch with you toward the end of the week."

That afternoon he visited representatives of the three faiths in the little town that had been a peaceful village before industry moved in. Though they were all definitely sectarian, each gave him just one name. Nobody could be as good as Mrs. Day, they said, for managing in the best way with the newcomers. When he discussed the matter with Miss Delancy she agreed enthusiastically with their choice.

Sitting in an old rocking chair, Mrs. Day was paring potatoes in her large, sunny kitchen when Mr. Wilson knocked on her door. She had seen him get out of his car with the USO sticker on the windshield and she knew from her talks with Miss Delancy who he was though she was not sure of the nature of his errand now. She was glad, however, that they were to have more help in their community.

"Coming," she called cheerfully to the man at the door, and turned up the fire under the tea-kettle. A warming cup of tea with some of her little spice-and-honey cakes would be very much in order for this gentleman who had come to work with them on their new problems.

Mrs. Day was a woman well past middle age who had been accustomed all her life to putting her hand to any useful job she saw needing to be done. Her husband was veterinarian for the community and since the farmland to the north-east was rather more prosperous than most, they had been comfortably well-off for years. Mrs. Day always did her own work even though they could easily afford a hired girl. She liked the feeling that her house was a going-concern under her own hand.

She had always lived in the town but had never supposed it was the center of the universe. In this she knew she was different from many of her friends. Their sleepy little community had had no warning of what the war was to do to it. Suddenly they learned that the Government had bought up many square miles of the poor farm land extending in a balloon-shaped bulge to the southwest. Most of these marginal farmers had been only too glad to sell, her husband told her. Some stayed on in the neighborhood to work in the powder plant. Others climbed on trains bound for distant relatives or got gas from the ration board under the permanent-change-of-residence clause.

Within a matter of weeks their town, instead of being the center of a large rural area, became a side issue to the great construction project six miles out of town.

Manpower catapulted in. Individuals and families lived in any sort of shelter they could find: tents, shacks, lean-to's, extra cots in the jail, in the firehouse, and some even in chicken houses. A central telegraph office was set up in a trailer, the rapidly constructed railway spur called the new Plant terminus by the town's name and suddenly the name became widely publicized in connection with employment opportunities—though Mrs. Day noticed that nothing was said about the lack of housing or the soaring cost of living that made heavy inroads even on good wages.

Immediately everything the town had to offer in the way of stores and commercial recreation—two movies and a bowling alley—was monopolized by the new population. All this began in the spring and by the end of the summer Mrs. Day saw that still another town facility—the public school—would be crowded up to and beyond capacity. She and Miss Delancy talked the matter over and agreed that a campaign must be begun for an additional school to help accommodate these new arrivals. Another school-connected situation they knew needed to be watched was the way the high-school students were signing up for night shifts at the Plant. School in the daytime and work at night was a strenuous schedule.

Mrs. Day had gone out to the trailer camp one day with Miss De lancy when she was disturbed about the garbage disposal since rats were becoming prevalent again. They talked to the camp manager who took them over to a neat trailer owned by a Mrs. Kroger. On that first occasion a flash of understanding had passed between the two housekeepers that had made them trust each other from that time on.

Since then Mrs. Kroger had spent more than one Sunday afternoon at Mrs. Day's and Mrs. Day had dropped in for supper at the trailer. On these occasions each guest had frankly admitted some hostility on the part of her acquaintances. Some of the townspeople said flatly they did not approve of these "women in pants." Others merely commented that the newcomers were not "their type." On the other hand the new population were apt to refer to the local residents as snobs and gougers.

If Mrs. Day had felt she had any right to personal complaint—which she didn't, what with the war going on and so many people tragically involved—it would have been that there was never any quiet any more. The town was awake all night. The Plant was running on three shifts which meant that one large group of workers had to eat and find what amusement they could between midnight and dawn. There was never a complete let-up to the noises of a restless population and the street lights and many electric signs blazed away all night. After a while, Mrs. Day grew accustomed to cotton in her ears and an old black silk scarf tied over her eyes. But sleep under those conditions never seemed to her wholly relaxing and she wondered how workers at the Plant, whose sleeping conditions could be no better than hers and probably were worse, could continue to do painstaking work and take the maximum care required by dangerous explosives.

Some of these things she discussed with Mr. Wilson that day as they drank their tea and he ate generously of her special little sugarless cakes. Mr. Wilson did most of the talking and his hostess sized him up accordingly. On the whole she thought he had common sense, and saw the major problems clearly.

"Where does the USO get all the workers that are needed to go into these new factory districts, Mr. Wilson? It must take years of training for a person to know how to come into a strange place the way you and Miss Delancy are having to and take hold in such a way as to get results." As soon as she made the inquiry she could see that this was a favorite subject of his.

"One thing the USO has prided itself on is using all the specialists it can get. The six Agencies composing the USO all had trained personnel of course before the war. Some of their workers were of draft age but many were older and the Agencies made them available, wherever possible, to tackle such jobs as these in industrial communities—where previous experience was required."

"Beside having to handle both the newcomers and the native settlers, what other main problems are there?"

Mr. Wilson, with such an appreciative listener, warmed to his subject. "I've been in this work for fifteen years and I think the most delicate problem of all—and it's magnified in time of war—is for the recreation or welfare worker to hold a careful balance between friendliness with labor and friendliness with management. You need the co-operation of both sides but each one will suspect you if you lean a little mite too far one way or the other."

Then seeing that time was getting on Mr. Wilson came to the point and asked her if she would teach in the trolley car Sunday School.

She thought it over for several minutes rocking evenly back and forth in the old rocker. "I'm just wondering," she said presently when Mr. Wilson was about to bring up further arguments, "whether there aren't some well-qualified teachers in the trailer camp itself. Would you like me to take it over for the first few Sundays and see what local talent I may be able to unearth?"

Rapidly the Federal Recreation Building that was to house the USO club was being pushed to completion. Miss Delancy knew it was important that the club itself become a symbol for the community. If the newcomers and the older residents could both have a hand in planning for its use and so feel it was their own club, gains already made might be consolidated and extended.

Suddenly there was a new development at the Plant: women were put on the explosives production line and at once additional women began pouring in by the hundreds. Miss Delancy read the Plant supervisor's confidential description of the sort of women workers he preferred:

Women who weigh close to 200 pounds, because their nerves are steadier.
Women with home ties, because they have more sense of responsibility and are less likely to be hunting excitement in their free time.
Women who are comfortably housed and free of worry, because they tire less quickly.
Women with no temperament.
Women with intelligence, because the job is monotonous.

Not many weeks after Mr. Wilson's arrival, the club was formally opened and regular programs were under way. He and Miss Delancy worked quietly but steadily to secure its acceptance as an integrating factor. Every effort they could make toward friendly community of interests among the conglomeration of people living in this industrial area was important.

One complicating factor was the way the shifts were changed. They would think they had made final arrangements involving certain people and then discover that these people had to sleep those particular hours because they had been transferred to a different shift. Both she and Mr. Wilson were anxious to hold a swingshift dance and they wanted the people working on this shift to have as much say as possible in the way the dance was run. But trying to have committee meetings with them at the hours the people thought of as natural was complicating, to say the least, to a "normal" working day.

Relatively this was a minor matter, Miss Delancy knew. The really big problem here that she had not encountered elsewhere was the danger of explosion. So far they had had no serious accidents, but she was aware of tension among the workers. Soon after her arrival she had talked to a man who had charge of loading bags with high explosives. He had told her he never used women on the line until he had to. "Someone always burns," he said, and he hated to think of women being hurt.

For other work such as weighing charges of black and smokeless powder, three girls and a supervisor occupied one compartment which was steel walled, explosion proof. These compartments were small, light, well ventilated, with the floors painted red so that any spilt powder would show. Working under such conditions took its toll in taut nerves. Enjoyable recreation after hours assumed almost the proportions of a safety measure.

Gradually as the USO extended its work, its operating committee grew stronger and more representative of all interests involved: a man from the public relations department of the Plant, one of the town councilmen, a rabbi, the president of the Service Club, a Catholic priest, two ladies from the Women's Club, including Mrs. Day, and several workers at the Plant including Mrs. Kroger.

This group was fairly alert to changes taking place in Plant personnel and as the housing projects were completed and more and more families moved into them, the operating committee felt something should be done for the younger teen-age boys and girls.

Mr. Wilson talked to Burt Kroger about it. Miss Delancy mentioned the matter to a couple of attractive and capable sixteen year old girls and it was not long before the Plant-teeners were formed, including young people up to draft age who would pay a quarter, receive a membership card, and agree to the few rules their own committee set up.

Under the sponsorship of a joint committee from the Men's Service Club and the Women's Club, the Planteeners asked for use of the USO club on an off-night each week. They would pay the expense of whatever entertainment they put on, they would clean up afterwards, and they would agree to the usual club rules. At the end of a couple of months they had nearly two hundred members.

Miss Delancy was as careful as was Mr. Wilson to be friendly to both management and labor but to be identified with neither. Only occasionally did some individual try to make her "take sides." One such instance occurred during an afternoon when a small group from the old residents, the new housing project, and the trailer camp were working on plans for a State Party. In setting up the committee Miss Delancy had selected three townspeople who had been born in three different states and had then hunted around until she found congenial newcomers from the same three. Their interests in common had worked like a charm and they were developing all sorts of schemes to extend the State idea into a very gala party.

Suddenly they were interrupted by a loud and surly voice in the little entrance hall. "They can run their old plant without me. I'm through with this whole town. Nobody in it but liars and cheats. I can't get out of it too fast to suit me! Where's the woman runs this joint? I want her to get me out on the next train leaving."

A moment later a worried looking Junior Hostess appeared and Miss Delancy went back to the front door with her.

"I'm one of the people in charge here," she told the belligerent young man. "I'll be glad to do anything I can."

"Then buy me a ticket to Detroit."

"If you'll come into my office I'll look up the schedule for you."

"I know the train schedule. All I want from you is the money."

"But we don't buy tickets for people."

"I was told if folks get stuck, you lend 'em the fare."

"In rare cases we do. But you aren't stuck, are you? Don't you work at the Plant?"

Their talk was extended. He admitted having had a job but claimed he had not been paid what the Plant's agent had promised him, though he had been paid what his contract specified. He asked again, though less belligerently, for enough money to get to Detroit. When she said the USO had no money for such purposes he asked if she knew any other place where he could get a job.

Miss Delancy gave him the names of several small employers who she knew needed men and saw no more of him for a couple of days though she heard indirectly that he was working for one of the men on her list.

The third day he was back asking again for money for the trip.

"But you'll have earned it by the end of the week."

"I know but I can't wait that long."

Then he broke down and told her the whole story. He hadn't told his wife he had been discharged from the Army. "She doesn't even know I'm back in this country. I didn't mean she should ever know. I thought I'd been through too much, seen too much ever to go near her again or be with our little girls. But now I know I gotta get home—if she'll have me. That's what I *have* to know. Now will you give me the money?"

Miss Delancy thought a minute. "Why don't you send your wife a telegram telling her you're back in this country and hope to be able to get home in a week or ten days? Tell her it will be wonderful to see her and the children—if you want to say that. And end up by asking her to telegraph you here."

The return message came quickly. Whatever it was, it seemed to make a new person of the belligerent young man. "Thanks," he said flushing a little at his own happiness. "Now I can *really* work!—and go home with some spare money in my pocket."

The war was over and Mrs. Day was in her same old rocker peeling potatoes and thinking of the headlines in the evening paper. She had been reading about the UN and some of their problems had seemed curiously familiar to her. This business of getting along with different people of different backgrounds, with different wants, with different ways of looking at things—she knew a little first-hand about that.

For them in this town, as all over the country, the first responsibility had been to win the war. Now the single responsibility was to work out ways for peace that would deserve to last.

Sitting there in her kitchen from which she could see the former USO club that the town was taking over as a permanent recreation center—sitting there and thinking of the planning and the forbearance and the generous give-and-take that had been necessary to make and keep that club running right, she wondered if working-things-out didn't involve much the same things on any level.

And the feeling came to her—hardly a formulated thought—that a country could only work things out with other nations on a durable basis as its people were able to work things out among themselves.

With This Ring

During the five years I was a USO club director the best helper I had with weddings was a lanky GI named Ambrose.

Ambrose wasn't one to talk about himself. When anybody asked him what they were doing for him at the Army hospital just up the hill he'd mumble something about "spring housecleaning after a long winter" and then get going on some curious yarn with a dry joke sandwiched into the telling.

Everybody liked having Ambrose around the club. Guess it was because he seemed pleased to be there himself, not shouting pleased, but content like he'd been coming a long time and had finally arrived.

First time I remember seeing him was one Saturday when the thermometer was outdoing itself: 98, 99, and by mid-morning, 101. You moved slow, I can tell you. But move you had to because, in addition to everything else, there was to be a wedding late that afternoon.

"How about one of you men grabbing hold of the other end of this davenport?" I suggested to the nearest ping-pong players. "Got to get it out of the way of a wedding."

"How about two of us grabbing hold of both ends?" countered the tall, thin one who turned out to be Ambrose.

"Swell! Guess the alley's the only place to put it."

It was a close thing getting it through the kitchen door but they made it with much joshing as to who was carrying the most weight. In the blazing sun of the alley the yellow upholstery took on a glaring brightness.

Both boys sat down on the davenport just for the fun of being so luxuriously seated in an alley and it not being a day to hurry about anything, even weddings, I sat down too.

"Pass the iced drinks, James," drawled Ambrose sliding comfortably down on his spine and crossing his long legs. "Who's getting married?"

I told him but he didn't seem to be listening. There was a queer looking-off expression on his face. "Let's make it a pretty wedding," he said suddenly. "I'll go get a whole mess of smilax and rig up a bank of it for them to stand against." I said, Go to it, and then Ambrose really got into action.

All the rest of the day everybody who stuck his or her nose inside the club was given a job. Generous ropes of smilax were looped across the front end of the club. More slender ones marked off the ceremony area. From somewhere came two immense white candles in handsome candlesticks which Ambrose placed against the smilax bank.

"Now you girls chase along home," he ordered the Junior Hostesses an hour before the ceremony was due to start. "You gotta put on long dresses. No use fussing," he interrupted the protests. "I know it's a hundred and eight but the men are going to button up their collars and wear ties and necks get a lot hotter than ankles do. So scram!"

"How come you know how to plan so well?" I asked curiously.

"I've thought about weddings such a lot." He said it as a man might say he'd gone all out for minerals or for birds or for philosophic stuff. "No, I'm not married," he guessed the question in my mind. "My interest's more general. It's funny but when you make yourself think about people getting married you somehow begin seeing them again as individual folks. It makes you remember there's a world where people are free to go their own personal ways." He broke off and I let there be a pause.

"For eighteen months," he told me then, "planning weddings in my head was my favorite sport." His smile was a little lopsided. "It's crazy the hobbies a guy'll go for—in a German prison camp."

CHAPTER IX

Service to Negroes

Mrs. Ellen Douglas, a well-dressed, pleasant looking Negro woman in her early forties, thanked the elderly landlady who showed her to her room. It was too good to be true that she had arrived at last. For thirty hours she had been riding in a day-coach. She could hardly believe that in a few minutes she would be able to wash her face in hot water and stretch out full length on a bed.

"You won't be needing water in your pitcher right off, will you?" There was an anxious note in the old Negro woman's voice.

Mrs. Douglas started to say, yes, she certainly would, then noticed that her landlady—she must be seventy at least with a sweet face and tight white hair—was still out of breath from their climb up two flights.

"Norman, my grandson, will bring it up when he gets home from school. But if you're in a hurry I can bring a small pailful myself."

"Don't think of such a thing. I'll take a nap first and clean up later."

"Then I'll be going back downstairs." The old woman turned away. Mrs. Douglas starting to close the door saw the stairway had no light except what came through her room. Swinging the door far open, she stood waiting, her hand on the knob, until the old woman reached the floor below. Then she moved her bags across the clean, bare floor, closed and locked the door.

With the turning of the key she let her usually erect carriage relax a little and wearily sat down on the side of the bed. Beneath the thin mattress the weak springs sagged into a hammock. Never mind, the place was clean.

Pulling herself up, Mrs. Douglas took off her small brown hat with the nicely curved brown and white feathers, put it on the shelf of the shallow closet, then glancing in the cracked mirror, smoothed the close upward swirl of her hair. For a moment she gazed into the glass, past her own reflection into memories beyond the room, memories of the days when her husband was living and their son, a flier now in the South Pacific, had been growing up in their little house, a rented house but furnished with all their own things. She thought of the beech tree in the yard, the plant shelf in the living room window, and the shining conveniences in the white and green kitchen.

Then with a quick movement she whirled to face the room, to see it exactly as it was, to realize fully the worst so there could be no later disillusionment. It was better not to fool yourself about the place to which you would be coming home night after night at the end of a long day's work at the USO.

The room was twice again as large as the bed. Under the little mirror was an oak washstand with a grey enamelled bowl and pitcher—the one Norman would presently be filling. The rest of the furniture was a card table and a straight, wooden chair. They would do for her typewriter and the record sheets she would be keeping as club director. But she would have to get herself a piece of furniture with drawers.

Could anything worth looking at be seen from her window? She pushed it up, felt it start to fall under her hand, and propped it with the stick she found lying on the sill. The window opened against a brick wall near enough so she could have touched it without leaning out. Without leaning out also she caught an acrid scent on the cold wind—the unmistakable odor of garbage too long uncollected. *Have engaged best room available* had run the telegram.

A few months before Mrs. Douglas's coming a disturbing incident had occurred in town. She had read the following description of it:

One hot, rainy Sunday afternoon in July the town was crowded with soldiers. The white soldiers were congregated in and about the Servicemen's Club run by the local USO Council where ladies from one of the churches were sponsoring a Snack Hour. Many of the local girls were present to help with the entertainment. The approach of each shower would drive a crowd of soldiers back into the club where the noise from the large pedestal fans seemed to compete with the roar of the rain. Jews, Catholics, and Protestants were all of them breaking bread together, all of them white.

With the Negro soldiers in town that afternoon it was different. They were congregated down the hill toward the station on a street where one little fourth-class cafe was open to them. It was short on food and its beer was not even cool. Groups of Negroes in khaki leaned and squatted about under the rusty corrugated tin shelters that covered the sidewalks in front of the closed shops. From the hot, paved streets the steam rose steadily.

One of these Negro soldiers, tall, intelligent and handsome, found this Sunday afternoon experience disgusting. With nothing else to do he walked into the little crowded cafe and called for a bottle of beer. His complaint about its being hot was answered with an apologetic assurance from the manager that the town could not get enough ice. As he drank the bottle of hot beer, he was jostled by other soldiers who pushed themselves against one another trying to get something cool to quench their thirst.

By the time he had emptied the bottle, his feeling of disgust had become one of strong resentment. He slammed the empty beer bottle down on the crude bar and shoved himself rudely through the crowd of perspiring Negro soldiers to the front door. His new regulation shirt had begun to stick to his shoulders and neck. With long, swift strides he walked in the warm rain toward the bus station. Camp at its worst was better than this damn town, he had concluded, so he was going back.

The bus station was also crowded so he stood outside and waited. Leaving early, he thought, would give him a better chance to get a seat or standing room at least. But disappointment awaited him. The first bus was filled with white passengers. The second bus, an old worn-out model, had been parked in the rear of the station and the angry Negro soldier had failed to notice the whiny feminine voice that announced it over the P.A. system. He saw a crowd of Negroes rushing in that direction and hurried along. The bus door closed with a slam just as he was about to catch it with his right hand.

Furious, he let out an oath with all the vehemence he had accumulated during his day of disappointment. A quick, unexpected jerk caught his left arm and whirled him completely about. He was facing a policeman. The records do not show who hit first but a terrific fight took place before the MP's arrived.

On the following Monday, early in the day, two of the town's prominent Negro citizens were enjoying coffee in the pharmacy. One was telling the other about the fight. "It wouldn't have happened if we had had some place for our colored soldiers to be entertained," one of them remarked. "That's what we need," agreed the other.

Apparently white leaders had agreed also, including the mayor and the president of the Men's Club, both of whom were members of the local USO Council. A little money was voted by the town and a few Negro men and women from the largest church were asked to see what arrangements could be made for renting some place to hold a dance and for engaging a small orchestra.

So successful was this preliminary entertainment that the Army asked if more extensive and more permanent facilities could not be provided. The only building of any size in the Negro community was the old abandoned mortuary, half filled at the time with scrap paper. The salvage people cleaned it out and the Negro group organized a show—with all-Army talent—to raise money for furnishings. Tickets were fifteen cents each and enough was cleared to buy an old juke box and a dilapidated living room set which the committee re-covered with stout material purchased at a ten cent store.

It soon became apparent, however, that a full-time person would be needed to manage the place, superintend the renovations, and arrange the programs. Other problems beside recreation needed attention. The USO Council appealed to the National USO and in due course a Negro club was authorized. It was at this point that a letter went to Mrs. Douglas, then assistant director in a club in another section of the country, asking her to be the director.

She accepted reluctantly. In one sense the new job would be a promotion. On the other hand her old club, located in a reputedly "liberal" city, gave opportunity, she felt, for developing new patterns of inter-racial work. The situation there had been evolving over a period of months. In the early days when Negro troops were first stationed in the nearby post, some of them had come to the one and only USO along with the white soldiers. To make the Negro troops feel more at home the local USO Council had asked her to join the staff on a part-time basis while she finished the work for her Master's degree. Her duties had not been heavy because most of the boys wanted nothing more than to look at magazines, write letters, play pool, or bowl, and facilities for these activities were ready at hand. By most people the attendance of Negroes at the club had been accepted in matter of fact fashion.

In due course here as in other places, the question of mixed dancing arose. Mrs. Douglas knew the matter had been managed differently in different places. In some, such dancing had been continued to the extent that Negro couples and white couples danced at the same parties. In other places the USO had made provision for two clubs, if necessary. Some communities, she knew, had concluded there were many Negroes who preferred a separate USO, though one reason for this preference might have been their treatment in white clubs.

These varying experiences in other places were being duly weighed by the local USO Council. There was much frank—and some heated— discussion. Pressure was brought to bear on her personally from various quarters. She had done her best to steer a middle course knowing that if too much was demanded the whole program might be lost. On the whole, she believed, facing this situation candidly was increasing general understanding. And when she resigned her position to take the directorship of the new club in a different section of the country, she knew there were leaders in this community she was leaving—both white and Negro—who would continue to think through the problems of segregation and of integrated procedures.

It would be due to such far-sighted and realistic facing of facts that substantial gains would be continued into the post-war period. Already as camps were closing there were evidences of this. Only recently she had heard of a sizeable town in the mid-west that had appropriated funds for the continued financing of both white and Negro recreation centers (formerly USO clubs) for the benefit of the white and Negro citizens of the city. And in a little southern town, before the USO pulled out, the Negro Board of Education had raised sufficient funds to provide for the continued operation of the building as a community center for Negroes—the only one within a radius of a hundred miles. Undoubtedly when the war was over and all USO clubs gradually closed, there would be other and even more impressive holdovers in communities that needed continuing welfare and recreation facilities. Also there would be other long-run gains. The USO would leave in many places the beginning of joint planning between white and Negro citizens for over-all community service. As a result of the way many USO Councils had functioned, she believed the distance between Negroes and white people had been perceptibly bridged and greater mutual understanding achieved.

Once her decision to accept the new offer was made, Mrs. Douglas lost no time getting to her assignment. There would be a lot to do before formal dedication of this new USO club would be in order—so much, in fact, that during the ensuing weeks the little room opening close to the brick wall saw her for scarcely more than the minimum hours required for sleep.

"Back home was nothing like this!"

Mrs. Douglas saw that the Negro corporal coming down the tall ladder made the remark more to himself than to her. The ladder stood against the exact center of the club's wall opposite the entrance door. Leaning from the top rung he had just tacked in place the sweeping folds of some red, white, and blue bunting on the right and of a USO banner on the left. Then he had paused to look around the big, gaily decorated room below him.

She smiled at his comment, knowing perfectly well that any pleasant place you put a lot of work into could be made to seem like home. She knew too that for some of the men who would come here the club would be a revelation in comfort and friendliness. Perhaps the corporal was one of them.

"Who all's coming to the dedication tomorrow night?" he asked. "The mayor?"

"No, the mayor can't be here. He told me so over the 'phone yesterday. But Mr. Lansing from the National USO is coming."

"How many civilians you expect to have? I hear two or three hundred boys are planning to come in from camp."

"We'll have at least one civilian to every two soldiers—maybe more."

"Big doings. Well, call on us for any help you need."

Humming lightly under his breath, he went off with the long ladder, getting a great deal of laughing assistance from some of the Junior Hostesses as they helped him and the ladder through the doors.

Mrs. Douglas, continuing with her work, thought the corporal's parting remark was typical of the way the boys had taken hold. Before the USO had officially authorized the club, the Commanding Officer at the Camp had offered to furnish "labor" if this building could be renovated and put in shape for the men's use. But the word fell far short of describing the patience and ingenuity that had gone into the place. They had had to tear down three partitions. Then had come the painting, every inch of the interior done by the men themselves. It was certainly a miracle that it didn't look patchy—the occasional panelling probably helped. They had entirely re-wired it too, the Army helping out with the materials.

While additional renovations were being made, now that the USO had taken over, Mrs. Douglas was busy recruiting more help from the Negro community. One of the greatest complications was that most of the women worked all day and any time given to the club's activities had to be taken from their responsibilities at home. It was amazing, however, the number of volunteer hours per week the record book was showing.

This was the first project in the town drawing help from the Negro community as a whole. It had been a new experience for the women of one church to work with the women of another, all of them making little favors for the opening night. Soon too the prospective club took on the characteristics of a community center. Already it was booked for three meetings a week: on Mondays at six for a First Aid Class; on Wednesdays for a meeting of Negro ministers, on Saturday mornings for a teachers' discussion group. And Mrs. Douglas, the only professionally trained social worker they had ever had, found herself called upon for advice and help in many matters that would have been referred to other agencies had they been available.

Over and over again in this beginning period things did not go well. The gap was so wide between what she wanted her volunteers to accomplish and their capacity. Now and then she found impressive natural abilities and she put them to work with enthusiasm, watching them develop under responsibility and in response to a minimum of suggestion from her. But with the rank and file it was slow work. Most of them had had only the most limited social life. Many had never taken part in anything that could fairly be called "recreation."

When soldiers came to town with a few hours leave and a longing to fill them with something that would distract them from military routine, what would they find? Almost nothing except what the USO club could offer them. Not even moderately good restaurants were open to them, no movies, nor general shopping privileges. To the Negroes who had grown up in these conditions this was nothing new but the camp outside the town was training men from all sections of the country.

Every day these men as they came to help plied her with questions. Would it be possible to buy a hamburger here and a glass of milk?— My wife at home needs some advice about the kids. Could you tell me what sort of organization to refer her to?—Is there any place where another fellow and me could listen to these records?—How can a man learn to jitterbug when the girls don't know how themselves? Couldn't we all get together and have a class?—Know anybody has a piano so a bunch of us could do some harmonizing?— Sure would be swell to talk to some older businessmen about what's cooking in the way of jobs after the war. How about arranging something like that for us some night?

It was to help deal with such questions and needs as these, as well as to provide mass recreation for crowds, that Mrs. Douglas had to train her volunteers.

Work with the girls was planned with special care. To become a Junior Hostess they were required to attend several training classes. Mrs. Douglas soon found their social contacts had been so limited in many instances that she had to begin with simple fundamentals of courtesy. Most of the girls were so anxious to learn the right way to conduct themselves as hostesses that they made good progress and entered with high spirits into the party she gave them at the end of their training course: a "Bad Taste Party" to which each wore something unsuitable for a club dance. Then, at the close of the evening, each changed into appropriate clothes for wearing on dedication night.

With the help of an eighteen year old girl—Evelyn Jones—who had a good soprano voice, a Glee Club was organized with two-thirds soldier talent and the rest Junior Hostesses. Pending completion of the club building they practiced in the basement of the nearest church. Hardly did they have their stride when they were asked to make a tour of all the churches to help raise funds in the current Red Cross drive.

The hardest single problem, next to organizing the club itself, was finding decent and clean places for soldiers' wives to live in. Stubbornly Mrs. Douglas stuck to her standards of decency and cleanliness. If a room did not qualify on those two points, she refused to list it. But she had had to forego two other standards with which she had come to town: running water and sewage disposal.

Often she wished she could consult the USO Council as a group. Of course she could telephone various members of the Council individually. They would advise her pleasantly enough (calling her "Ellen" as a matter of course, never "Mrs. Douglas"). What was really needed, however, was thorough discussion of some of the problems by interested people sitting down together with all the facts before them. She knew that of the three hundred or more Negro USO's in the country, Negroes were members of a majority of the Councils. But no slightest indication had ever been given here that Negroes were to be represented. In fact she had heard second-hand that the president of the Council, Mr. Smith, had said he could see no possible value in any such arrangement.

The last day before the dedication ceremonies everybody helped. In the auditorium the corporal on the high ladder hung the last of the bunting. Other men from camp came later to put the final touches on their two ping-pong tables. The tables were terribly heavy to move— and moved they would have to be when the center of the floor was cleared for dancing—but everybody was enormously proud of them.

In the pantry the dishes that had been donated to the club before it became a USO—two plates from one family, three cups from another, platters from a third, and so on—were being freshly washed and stacked in piles according to size. In the kitchen beyond, a large airy room with bright designs stencilled by some of the school teachers on the white brick walls, extensive preparations were going forward. Though they talked little about it, all the workers knew there were no clean, good restaurants in town available to the Negro troops. So the Snack Bar at this club was bound to be more important than it was in many other USO's.

"Taste the fruit punch, Mrs. Douglas?"

"You speak as though I'd be doing you a favor!"

The punch-maker beamed, feigning culinary modesty. But Mrs. Douglas, slowly sipping the delicious cold drink, knew that not for anything in the world would its maker share her cherished recipe!

The refreshment committee was preparing for four hundred and all the materials had been donated. Mrs. Douglas had tried to reimburse the donors—at least, to the extent of funds budgeted for the purpose. "Not this time," they had said. "Not for our dedication." And by the half-cupful the necessary sugar continued to come in together with cookies, pies, and cakes, and now and then a cup of lard for frying frankfurters.

"You're wanted on the 'phone, Mrs. Douglas."

She ran. It was the businesslike, slightly rasping voice of Mr. Smith, chairman of the Men's Club and of the USO Council. "About tonight, Ellen. I'll bring Mr. Lansing to the club at eight o'clock sharp. Then you give me a ring—I'll be at home—when your little ceremony is over and I'll drive around for him."

Mr. Lansing, a national director of the USO, finished a hearty lunch in the diner and went back to his seat in the chair car. He had the afternoon before him now to think through the best line to take in dedicating this new Negro club. He was conscious of agreeable energy at the prospect.

For a man well over fifty he was feeling very fit this afternoon— which was just as well since he had a stiff job ahead of him. What disconcerted Mr. Lansing's business colleagues was that in spite of his financial and executive achievements, his schedule of activities always included stiff jobs ahead. It was almost as though he had a knack for withdrawing from situations once they became routinized and placid, moving over into other fields where the hurdles were a little higher than any he had previously taken. They were always saying it was nobody's fault but his own that Lansing was forever getting himself involved in problems. And since that was their attitude Mr. Lansing didn't bother to explain to them that he considered the country was up against as many frontiers as it had ever been and that everybody who could spare a little energy ought to help shoulder the rugged jobs involved.

Taking a small pad and pencil from his inside pocket, he pulled his vest down over scarcely any bulge, smiled absently at the brilliant fall landscape streaming by the window and began to jot down notes. Had he known himself as well as some others knew him he would have realized that his smile and the steady state of being from which it sprang were going to cut more ice in the job ahead than anything he was apt to write on the pad.

However, facts carefully lined up were seldom superfluous. They served to orient you and Mr. Lansing was a firm believer in starting from where you were—not from where you wished you were—when action had to be taken.

First things first, decided Mr. Lansing, writing on his pad. The primary responsibility of the USO to Negro citizens in this country was to provide Negro servicemen with welfare and recreation services. The USO's articles of incorporation had seen to that when they explicitly stated that service was to be to *all* servicemen. It was the organization's aim and energetic endeavor to provide them with the same or comparable services. In this for a variety of reasons, noted Mr. Lansing with candor, the USO was not always successful though the per capita cost of the work for Negroes was higher than for whites.

Mr. Lansing laid his pad and pencil on the window sill and unhurriedly removed the cellophane wrapping from a special brand of cigar. Searching his pockets for a match, he thought the war has brought some of America's racial problems into new focus and added to their geographic distribution. All of these problems are important in the long run and in a general sense to the country as a whole.

"No smoking in here, sir." It was the conductor.

"Sorry. Of course not. I forgot where I was." He looked around for an ashtray against which to extinguish his cigar. Finding none he used the sole of his shoe.

The thing of real significance was that because of the war the USO was able to do things in the bi-racial picture that on-going social agencies could not so easily do. There was something about an "emergency" that loosened people and situations up. Maybe it was because emergencies were supposed not to last very long. People were willing to take chances, to try new things under the stress of war.

About a tenth of the men in the Army were Negroes, thought Mr. Lansing crossing his knees the other way and wishing he could smoke. But if he went into the smoking room somebody would be sure to talk to him and he had to bring, uninterrupted, the whole picture fresh before his mind. Somebody might even demand why the USO didn't take advantage of its position and of the war emergency to come out unequivocally against segregation.

He could answer that one in his sleep, so many times and so hotly had it been put to him. It was amazing, he reflected gazing unseeing out of the window, how many people there were who respected integrity in individuals but thought an organization was free to do anything it could "get by with." He did not agree. An organization—in this case the USO—had a very definite integrity to maintain. It owed its continuing existence to the public who supported it with money and with volunteer services. And what had those people given their money and effort for? Not for social reform—no matter how desperately needed—but simply to help out the boys with "a home away from home." The USO was a service organization pure and simple.

There were, however, certain other considerations fairly in the picture. So vast was the scope of this work that varied opportunity was given to learn how theory could be realized in practical situations. Also there was definitely a learning area between the two "musts" that the USO had had to accept: the necessity of furnishing morale-building services to their Negro clientele, on the one hand; and on the other, the necessity of respecting the mores of the community concerned while giving leadership and providing services on as democratic a basis as possible.

Whenever Mr. Lansing used that expression, "the mores of the community," he paused for the shout of derision he had learned to expect from the absolutists, the people who believed that social change could be successfully superimposed if it could be done with a sufficiently firm hand. In his opinion these extremists had an obsession rather than a conviction based on experience. Each of the religious agencies in the USO had its own program for improvement of race relations. Each believed implicitly in the importance of individual personality. They were aware, however, that segregation was not merely a matter of attitude in some places. They knew that compulsory separation of Negro and white people in public transportation or in schools or in other public or semi-public places was a matter of law in more than a quarter of the states.

In these states, if the USO was to render badly needed services to Negro servicemen, it had no choice but to operate under the law as it stood. Its opportunity lay in bringing to the general public's attention the type and extent of immediate need and in demonstrating what could be done on the positive side. On the whole, Mr. Lansing felt, the USO had exercised considerable perspicacity in using the opportunity.

Well, that was that. The thing now, in connection with this dedication tonight was to make it count for as much as possible. How to manage that he would have to decide when he got there.

Feeling that he'd given himself a fairly satisfactory work-out by way of preparation, he got up and marched down the aisle to the adjoining clubcar.

"Whisky and soda, sir?" inquired the steward softly.

"No," said Mr. Lansing shortly, already turning over in his mind a little matter of approach that he might use this evening, "Buttermilk."

"Mr. Mayor, about the order of speaking at the club tonight—" Mr. Lansing paused, awaiting their full attention. Dinner was over at the Mayor's residence and Mr. Lansing had settled back in his chair with the excellent cigar that Mr. Smith, chairman of the USO Council, had given him. Of the other half dozen leading white citizens, one lit a pipe. The others were satisfied with cigarettes.

Through the blue haze the visitor looked briefly at each of them, then went on with easy matter-of-factness. "Suppose I lead off about the work of the USO in general. I thought I might also bring in a little about the ward parties we've begun to give in military hospitals—at the invitation, of course, of the Commanding Officer and in full co-operation with the Red Cross. This convalescent service is the newest thing we're doing."

He paused to tap the ash from his cigar. "It's interesting," he added thoughtfully, "that though the Army has continued some of the patterns of segregation, once a man is wounded, all the separation is over. The Purple Heart people are all treated alike, regardless of race, in the hospitals. It's almost as though—" His words had a quiet, impelling quality in the stillness of the room. "It's almost as though, once blood is shed, we can see with our own eyes that it's all bright red. Then," he interrupted himself, "I'll end up with a funny story— at least, *I* think it's funny. Let me tell it to you and see what you think." The warmth of his voice included them all as he asked for their opinion.

"It happened on the Mexican border. One of our Mobile Service trucks with the regular USO label—you know what it looks like: USO in the middle, three stars above and three below representing the six founding Agencies—anyway one of the Mobile units had been over the line on an errand and when the fellow started back, he found everybody being detained at the customs for some special reason. He had a couple of USO appointments he wanted to keep so he hailed an official—an old duffer he'd often seen before—and told him it would be bad if he were held up long.

"'Of course, of course,' agreed the customs officer. 'No reason why you shouldn't drive right through.' And he called to the man at the gate, 'Let that fellow through there. Can't you see he's a six-star General?'"

While everybody laughed, Mr. Lansing went steadily on. "Then suppose you speak next, Mr. Mayor. After that Mrs. Douglas might be willing to tell us something about the club activities she is planning. And then Mr. Smith—" bowing slightly toward the Council chairman, "perhaps you, as one of the inspirers of the club, will sign off for us."

Not waiting for their replies, Mr. Lansing added immediately that he was sorry he would not be able to linger afterward. He must catch a train back. In fact he was having the through-express flagged at the nearby junction. "I'm sure it will be all right," he added, "if all of us, as the guests of honor, go to the snack bar immediately from the platform and have our refreshments first. Then, Mr. Mayor, if your chauffeur, as you were kind enough to suggest, could drive me—"

She couldn't ask for the club to look any nicer, Mrs. Douglas thought in that fleeting moment between finishing preparations and the arrival of the honor guests. The new furniture, the good-looking draperies—not second-hand stuff but fresh and modern and just like the furniture and drapes of other USO clubs across the country— what a lift this equipment had given all of them! Those are for *us?* they had asked, not believing, when the shipping cases came. Their emphasis on the "us" had filled her with conflicting emotions—an impotent sort of rage, sadness, and a very present joy. But best of all tonight was her knowledge that there were so many others beside herself who were sharing in this proprietary pride. So many different people had had a hand in this achievement.

And the people themselves—so well-behaved and happy. That was partly due to the dignity and friendliness of the older men and women they had selected for the welcoming committee. It was for them to set the tone of the club as soldiers and civilians came trooping in the door.

Suddenly the ceremonies got underway with a rush. Mr. Lansing, leading the other seven honor guests to the platform, lost no time. They all stood for one verse of the "Star Spangled Banner" led by the Glee Club. Then Mr. Lansing told them about USO work, somehow making them feel a self-respecting and important part of something bigger than themselves. Naturally the Mayor couldn't live up to such a speech as that, thought Mrs. Douglas, but she felt he did well enough. Then she heard her own name called and her heart stopped altogether. But all Mr. Lansing wanted was for her to tell them about the things the club was going to do. Anybody could do that after all the thought they'd put into the plans. It was wonderful the way they cheered and clapped when she got through. She guessed Mr. Lansing would understand they were really applauding all they had achieved together. Then came Mr. Smith's closing remarks. After that the Glee

Club led them in singing "America, The Beautiful" and the ceremony was over.

The guests of honor walked down off the platform and over to the
snack bar at the side. The committee had everything ready for them.
Mrs. Douglas slipped outdoors to be sure their cars were at the curb
so they wouldn't have to wait. It was a clear evening and she stopped
for a moment to look up at the faintly luminous sky. What a night
it was—indoors, as well as out. She wondered if Mr. Lansing realized
the innovations he had brought about: white USO people—local
people—speaking for the first time from the platform of a Negro
club, then stopping for punch and sandwiches.

Now they were coming out. Mr. Lansing was smiling and so was
the Mayor in a deprecating sort of way as though he didn't want to
seem to take more credit than was due him. Mr. Lansing had managed to make them all proud. Mrs. Douglas could see it in their faces
as they lingered with him on the curb while the wind blew the trash
of the unkempt street about their well-polished shoes.

"Fine new club you have here," Mr. Lansing was saying to them.
"Your town is to be congratulated." When he saw her, he shook hands
and wished her great success.

Then he was gone in the Mayor's car. For a moment Mrs. Douglas
felt its going left more of a void than its physical absence from the
street. She shivered for there seemed to be a chill in the wind and the
last of the dried leaves, blown in from the distant gardens of the town,
whirled along the gutter with a scratching sound.

"Ellen—" she heard her name in Mr. Smith's slightly rasping businesslike voice. It so perfectly matched the bleakness of the moment
as to be no interruption. "There's to be a meeting of the Council in
my office tomorrow afternoon at three—"

"Yes?" She tried to hold the tone of her voice to neutral inquiry
but a sudden springing hope made the word sound eager.

"We would be glad if you would attend regularly hereafter as the
representative of this club."

She pressed her hands together hard to help hold back a shout. "Thank you, Mr. Smith. I shall be glad to come."

He nodded and drove off with the others in the remaining car.

Progress, she thought—what a relative word it was, measuring the distance from wherever you had been to the new place you moved ahead to. So she knew that here in this town progress had been made, that now a broader way was open for slow but steady betterment of racial understanding.

Suddenly the door of the club flung open and yellow light flooded to the curb. "Where are you, Mrs. Douglas?" A soldier and Evelyn Jones stood laughing in the doorway. "Come on in, can you? We need you to call the dances."

"Coming. Run along back. I'll be there in a minute."

This was no time for tears, hot behind her eyes. She took the minute to blink them back. Then with new buoyancy of spirit she walked quickly across the pavement into the warmth and light and promise of her club.

Candles in the Wind

I was working with the USO Mobile Service in the California desert that summer of '42 and one late afternoon all of a sudden my car went bad and there I had to sit until, fortunately, along came a sergeant who knew about engines. He fixed me up but he didn't like the looks of his handiwork any too well so he drove all the way in behind me though it was quite a piece out of his way.

Ten months later as I was getting ready to board a crowded day-coach in Tennessee, I heard somebody say, "Let me swing those bags on for you" and there was the desert sergeant. We were going the same way so we talked a bit and afterwhile he asked me if I'd be willing to write to him overseas. Said he was shipping out soon and didn't have much of a family here and anyhow he'd like to keep in touch, though he was just a kid and I nearly twice his age.

He was stationed in Ireland and I wrote to him regularly telling all the news from the States I thought he'd care to hear. Then one day he asked in his letter if I'd mind his sharing his mail with his buddies. It seemed he was living with a couple of fellows, one a Catholic and one a Jew and they got lonesome for word from home. So of course I said sure, go right ahead. I'd be proud to have you.

Then the first thing you know Christmas was coming on. And what do you think? Each of the three wrote me a separate letter and asked would I mind visiting services for them and then tell them how it was. I'd never been to a Jewish Friday evening service before but of course I went and they were so warm and friendly to me. Seemed to understand all about it when I told them why I'd come.

The Catholic boy wanted me to go to midnight Mass of course and I stood in line two hours and a half at St. Patrick's and afterward did what I could to convey the beauty of it. But I'm not a good enough writer, really.

It was a carol service the young sergeant wanted and I found a lovely one with candles and a lot of children, little ones and older ones and all in white.

It was grand of them, I thought, to want to celebrate that way even if they had to do it through another person. But the finest thing of all, I knew, when I heard about it afterwards, was their own Christmas eve. They were stationed in a barn that night—they'd moved on from Ireland to a combat zone. And a little before midnight an Army chaplain came around and asked did any of them want to pray that night. So they said they guessed they all would, if he would say the words. And then afterwards, because it was Christmas eve, you know, and they were just kids a good long way from home, they each lit a candle inside a sort of old iron oven that happened to be stored there in the barn. They made sure no light could show outside and each said his candle was for me because I was going to services in the States for them.

The rest of what they wrote me, I wouldn't hardly dare believe. I guess those boys just stayed too long in Ireland. But even so it was a fanciful thing for them to write down in a letter. What they said was that in the night they were ordered forward from the barn and a great artillery duel began, softening things up so they could move still farther on. Next day reenforcements brought word up their barn had been pounded flat but toward the middle of the wreckage had been a sort of oven thing and inside it three candles had been burning, their flames streaming, rather, in the open wind.

CHAPTER X

Toward New Civilian Living

John Richmond, gray-haired and thoughtful, slowly climbed the attic stairs of his house. His pace was due to preoccupation with a problem rather than to any lack of physical vigor for at sixty he dispatched as much work as he had for the last ten years. Walking over to a window under the eaves he gazed across business and residential roofs to a broad area several miles beyond the town limits. During most of the war it had been a training camp. Recently it had become a hospital.

In the change was a sign of the times. The war was over. Where men had trained for combat, they were now recovering for a return to civilian life. The hospital would have its effect on the town, he knew—less extensive than had been the impact of the training camp but in some ways more difficult to meet. Already the USO Council of which he was chairman, had met to discuss the matter.

His town was not alone in this new problem. Across the country many workers were realizing that there would be one more phase of USO work for those clubs—some 500 of them—operating near Army and Navy military hospitals. It was becoming clear that with the proper training, these USO's could assume a responsibility that military doctors were anxious to put upon them. What these doctors wanted was an easy transition for their patients from the hospital to civilian life. They needed a chance to do things by themselves in a non-military, non-hospital atmosphere or in small groups where the civilians were sufficiently impersonal but understanding.

These clubs near hospitals would be used also for other, though related, purposes. They would become friendly community centers for wives and mothers who came to visit their hospitalized men. In them, further, groups of selected Junior Hostesses would be trained to give parties at the hospitals when asked to do so by the Red Cross or the officer in charge.

For some clubs these hospital-connected activities would be new developments into which the regular program gradually moved. For others, as in his own town, they would come unexpectedly after a USO Council, seeing its nearby camp close down, had thought its job was done.

Only last week he had called their Council together, not without some groanings from volunteers who protested they had thought they could cross USO work off their list.

"The Red Cross is supposed to do hospitals," objected several.

"Inside the hospital itself, yes," he had agreed, "except, of course, for USO Camp Shows which bring in live entertainment and por-trait sketching artists. But some of these men are supposed to get out of the hospital grounds to stretch their legs and their minds. And," he forestalled another query, "they don't like to go to the public movies or other crowded places—especially the plastic surgery cases. They think they're being stared at. And they usually are."

There seemed nothing for it but to agree that the club should be reopened and this new job tackled, though enthusiasm among the members varied. It was decided that one person should be put in charge of all the work for hospitalized servicemen, whether done at the hospital upon proper request, or in the USO club. It was unani-mously left to John Richmond as chairman to find this person. He had made a wry face and asked what would happen if they didn't like his choice. They'd take a chance, they said.

And so they had, he remarked a little grimly now, gazing toward the hospital. He had known at the time whom he would appoint if given the power to do so and he had not changed his mind. He knew some would be surprised and those who wanted the job themselves— there were a few who did—might be sharply critical at first.

It was at infrequent moments like this when John Richmond decided something in his town, that his secure position in it came to his aid. His family had lived there ever since there had been a town— bankers, lawyers, or doctors and while they had possessed no such wealth as many newcomers, it was generally felt they were people whose opinions were sound above the average.

Opening the attic window to the fresh evening wind he took a deep breath and checked over in his mind the people who would like to be named chairman for the sake of the title. They were not the men and women who had shouldered the executive responsibilities for the USO when the camp load had been heaviest on the town. Of those who hoped he would single them out for the honor, some were out of a job and restless in the inconspicuousness of their present status, others were eager to do this work because of the emotional orgy they would make of it. Neither type of person did John Richmond intend to have in charge.

Well, this was the night, he thought now, having a look at his watch, for firing the opening gun in his campaign to set the work up properly. He was driving over to the hospital to see a Camp Shows performance and it was time he was getting under way.

Closing the window he made his way downstairs. He had told Tom and Anne Winter he would stop for them at half-past seven. This would hurry their dinner, he realized, for they were rich and stylish people. But opportunities to see a Camp Shows program were rare and he had built up his invitation considerably.

Tom Winter, though a relative newcomer—he had lived in the town only fifteen years—was a great friend of his. They went on fishing trips together. Lately he hadn't seen much of him because Tom was doing some hush-hush stuff for the Government.

His wife, Anne, had been a local girl, daughter of the druggist, and while some people thought she had changed since becoming Mrs. Winter, he didn't think so. At least her black eyes had as much gaiety as ever in them. Her sense of fun was not at anyone's expense. It was not as definite, as overt a thing as that—more of an emanation from an inward sense of delight. She was a good executive, too, quiet but observing. She had been head of their Civilian Defense and he had felt it was largely due to her unobtrusive skill that there had been a minimum of collisions between the vested interests involved in that program which, as directed by the Higher Ups, had been such a difficult blend of vagueness and military precision.

The Camp Shows performance scheduled for tonight was a variety program and John Richmond ushered in his guests just before the Master of Ceremonies took over. He was pleased to find, as the show went on, that it was an especially good troupe. The accordionist was a wizard, the girl who managed something of both tap dancing and ballet in such crowded quarters, elicited his hearty appreciation as she did that of the men. But it was a little blond comedienne with a soprano unexpectedly moving who brought the house down. In the midst of a storm of applause John Richmond heard a woman sob and turning hastily around to the door, near which he was sitting, he saw a nurse with her hands over her face, crying. He went over to her quickly thinking something serious must be wrong only to have an interne whose eyes also were unnaturally bright lay his hand on his arm.

"It's all right sir," the doctor assured him in a low tone. "It's just Jimmy."

John Richmond looked where he motioned and saw a great fuss being made over a youngster by all the patients within reach.

"The kid had nervous paralysis," explained the doctor blowing his nose. "When he heard that girl sing he forgot he couldn't use his arms and applauded. Boy, how he did clap!"

When the Camp Shows entertainment was over the Commandant invited the performers and guests to spend a little time talking to the boys. The first patient John Richmond spoke to had a USO Scrapbook lying on the blanket within easy reach of his hand.

"Where did you get that, son?" he asked.

"In Paris, sir. They gave a Scrapbook to every wounded man who was being flown home that trip. Nice and light to hold. Sure was good to see stuff from American magazines again!"

Presently when John Richmond saw his guests were engaged in conversation with a number of the patients, he slipped out and went into one of the wards where he had been told one of the Camp Shows sketchers was at work.

He found the artist sketching the powerful head of a Negro paratrooper though it was difficult to see how he could do so through the involved traction that was supporting both the man's arms and one leg.

"Who are you going to send the portrait to?" asked John Richmond. "It's going to be a beauty."

"To my wife, sir." Then he added with pride, "She's going to graduate from medical school next June."

When the artist had deftly caught the proud look that had crossed his subject's face at mention of his wife, he told them he had had a funny experience a few days before. In one of the other hospitals where he sketched there had been a problem patient—a boy named George whose hands had been badly burned. The doctors had done an expert job of repairing and had tried their best to get him to use his hands so as to gain strength and coordination. The boy refused, however, to make the slightest effort. He wouldn't try to shave. He wouldn't comb his hair. He knew his hands would never be any good, that the doctors were only fooling him.

The artist said he knew nothing about this background the afternoon he came into the ward to sketch and stopped by this boy's bed to ask if he'd like to have his portrait made. The boy made no reply, simply turned his head away, so the artist went on to the next man and got to work. When he had finished and was showing the picture, its subject said, "Look, mister, what's happened to George over there." The artist turned around and saw George, looking a little sheepish, sitting up in bed. He had shaved himself, combed his hair, and was now all ready to have his portrait made!

When John Richmond stopped at the Winters' house again an hour or so later, he said abruptly, "Tom, I want Anne to head our whole program for convalescents. Is this the time to ask her?"

"Well, I don't know. I think Anne had in mind resting up for awhile."

"I'll tell you the problem." Rapidly John Richmond told them the most important factors involved and his candid reasons for not wanting the work headed by certain types of people, no matter how efficient.

"Why do you want me?"

"Does she want this man-to-man, Tom?"

"She's pretty tough. Go ahead."

"Because you get things done without fuss but chiefly because you think living is a lot of fun."

Driving home, John Richmond felt well pleased with the evening's work. He was not greatly surprised that Anne Winter had accepted. He had done his best to make her see that this work with convalescents was part of a more extensive social improvement. As at the hospital servicemen were moving toward new civilian living, so was the country as a whole. Facility developed during the war for dealing with the well-being of individuals could not help but be a healthy and vital fact for the future.

Turning into his own side street he thought about the thousands of men and women across the country who had shown initiative through the USO in finding out what a boy needed during the war to bring out the best in him. Wouldn't their plain, everyday common sense tell them that peoples' welfare was more important than we'd ever before considered it in time of peace? Surely, also, many of them would know, because they'd seen evidence of it for themselves, that religion was a deeply rooted part of American life and that that over-all fact was more important than the differences between creeds.

"The USO," he concluded under his breath as he closed the garage doors, "has been a little sample of democracy in action with its variety, push, clumsiness, originality, resourcefulness, bickering, and solid achievement. Sometimes the USO has been bumptious and occasionally smug. But I do believe," he told himself feeling for his doorkey among the small change in his pocket, "I do believe that the people who've worked in it are going to see that there's a continuing social need for alertness and ingenuity and the sort of kindness that doesn't bog down in sentiment but gives a fellow just the lift he needs."

Around ten o'clock next morning, Mrs. Winter went around to the USO. The sign outside had never been taken down and John Richmond had told her that several days ago he had asked the old couple who used to divide the janitorial and laundry responsibilities between them, to open up and begin to make the club livable again.

As she went in now through the open front door her first impression was of a good fresh smell. Windows as well as doors stood open to the pleasant breeze and newly laundered curtains billowed back into the lounge. The slip covers too looked neatly tubbed.

Mrs. Winter absorbed this with unexpected pleasure, then looked about to find the place apparently in full swing. In four of the easy chairs were khaki figures with overseas ribbons, deep in the morning's papers. Not until later did she notice that each had some physical handicap. From the kitchen at the back came shouts of laughter, both girls' and men's. Apparently all you had to do to reactivate a USO was to open the door.

Two Navy nurses and two paratroopers looked around from the stove and smiled when she said "hello" from the kitchen doorway.

"Hope you don't mind our taking possession," one of the nurses said. "We couldn't find anyone to ask and it was too windy to have the picnic breakfast we had planned outdoors."

"We've been plotting for weeks," interrupted the other girl, "to get this day off, all of us together. We're sisters and we're marrying brothers. And here," with a dramatic flourish, "are the brothers!"

Mrs. Winter acknowledged the merry introduction in kind and said she hoped supplies weren't too short.

"Oh we brought everything. All we needed was a place."

As Mrs. Winter went back toward the front of the building she saw coming in the door a solid, wind-blown young woman with naturally brilliant coloring. In each hand she had a large suitcase.

"Hi!" said the girl. "Can I leave these bags here? My husband's up at the hospital. I have to find a place to stay. They're going to let me see him—maybe tomorrow."

"Better put your bags in the office. We've been closed here for awhile and the checking system isn't running yet."

Then she saw the girl was staring at her with a queer, fixed expression. "Gosh, ma'am," she stated her trouble flatly, "can you help me out somehow? His face's all mussed up. They're going to make the whole of it over and I'm as nervous as a girl seeing him for the first time. I'm afraid I won't be able to hide from him how the first look knocks me off my pins."

"Have you seen any of the wonderful plastic surgery they are doing at the hospital?"

"No'm."

"Maybe you'd feel surer about things if you did see some. The woods around here are just full of men in various stages of repair. Why don't you and I drive out toward the hospital? We'd be sure to see some of the boys walking in. It takes some time, you know, but they do look so much better when they're finished."

"That'd be swell. Not being so dumb about what to expect would make me a lot easier in my mind. Not but what I can take as much as the next," she added firmly. Then, less firmly, "Would you just call me 'Marge'? It'll help to hear my own first name."

Such was Mrs. Winter's initiation and the re-opened USO followed much these general lines as time went on. From early morning until eleven at night ambulatory patients dropped in and made themselves at home. The place was never uncomfortably crowded except on party nights. But neither was it ever empty. And in addition the relatives of patients made it their headquarters. All the people who carried responsibilities in the club were given careful training. Doctors and psychologists came down from the hospital to talk to them about the most effective services they could render.

Gradually, John Richmond observed, the USO took on a quality it had never had before—a sort of expectancy in the air. It was not the tension of imminent excitement. But something gentle, though not hovering, a breeziness that swept you pleasantly along. He was too much of a realist to think that such a characteristic was always at the forefront in the club. Too many different sorts of people came and went—both hostesses and guests. But time and again when he dropped in, he felt a definite lift in the place. It was as though the USO unquestioningly assumed that each of its guests was on his way to an interesting new phase of his life.

Just one new volunteer did Mrs. Winter herself add to the club: an old friend of hers whose arms had been badly burned when she was a little girl. For years her mother had made her wear long-sleeved dresses and gloves. But after her marriage her husband persuaded her to dress just like other people.

The first evening this woman was serving as hostess, a soldier came up to the table where she was helping a sailor hunt up some business addresses. Laying his badly damaged arm beside hers, the newcomer asked quietly, "How long did it take for the skin grafting job on yours? They're just beginning to work on mine." They both went on interestedly to discuss the new techniques in such repairs and when he made a move to go he said with a casualness that did not deceive the new worker, "Well, it hasn't kept you out of circulation, has it?"

In a sunny corner at the back of the building two sewing machines were set up for the use of young mothers who wished to make clothes for their youngsters. To increase their sense of homelike privacy, Mrs. Winter suggested to some of the men who used the club that they might make a four-winged screen from some lumber and building board she had managed to acquire. This was a popular undertaking and when the screen was nearly finished a GI reported he had a couple of artist buddies up at the hospital who'd be able to come to the club soon—maybe they'd do a paint job.

Different types of handicaps required somewhat different training for Junior Hostesses and the USO did not invite a group of blind boys to the club until a dozen competent girls felt themselves ready to handle the evening. At first they thought they would have a sit-down dinner party but after talking the matter over with two of the men from the hospital who went around with the blind patients, they decided to have an indoor picnic and let the boys cook hamburgers for themselves and for the girls who would be their dates for the occasion.

When the special guests for the evening arrived they "brailed" the kitchen first, getting the hang of the location and equipment including the extra electric grills the girls had installed. Then they set to work with onions, frying pans, and buns to be toasted.

"How about me making some flapjacks?" asked one burly fellow presently. "Have you got any pancake flour? Bet I can still flip 'em without a miss—not meanin' no pun, ma'am."

The derisive shout greeting his wit hardly sounded above the general racket and the sounds of frying. When one of their guests made a mismove and dropped something his well-trained partner refrained from picking it up but told him impersonally where it was. "The tablespoon's just by your right foot."

Then Mrs. Winter connected a small radio and dance music added its beat to the miscellaneous sound.

"How about dancing while our hamburgers simmer away?" said a girl. "I'm one of those who like their's well done."

"Me too. But I haven't danced since—"

"I can't do any of the new stuff either but there's almost six square feet of space over there by the refrigerator. Let's have a try."

"Do you suppose I still can?"

And more than one Junior Hostess who had gone through strenuous preparatory training had her reward that night in her partner's pleased remark, "Gosh, this is something!" when he found he could.

After they had eaten to the full extent of their capacity, had washed the dishes, and put the kitchen in order, they all walked across the street and spent the rest of the evening bowling.

There was a lot of coming and going at the club—men being discharged, new men or their families arriving. Marge took over for the new civilian arrivals. There was a heartiness about her, an out-in-the-open facing of what had to be faced that could not fail to put heart in anyone. And there was the fact too that if she could keep her chin up as she was obviously doing, anybody else ought to be able to, for her husband's face was undergoing one of the most extensive repair jobs undertaken at the hospital.

One day when a rather silly young girl was making a great fuss because her fiance's good looks were going to be "all spoiled" by the need for some plastic surgery on his ear, Mrs. Winter heard Marge give her a full description of what her husband was going through. "But how can you keep on loving him?" the girl demanded.

And Marge had answered, not too sympathetically, before she went on about her business, "It just happens, child, that I married a man, not a face."

It was Marge too who solved another problem that distressed some young mothers beyond its importance. There were articles in the current press about the reunion of overseas fathers and the youngsters they had never seen or had seen only as babies. There were melo-dramatic descriptions of the psychological hazard it was for the vet-eran when his child failed to recognize him.

One morning a young wife, conditioned by such tales, came into the USO in so jittery a state that it was plain to anyone that she would herself disturb the husband she was to be allowed to visit in two or three days.

"You scared your kid won't know his dad?" demanded Marge going straight to the heart of the difficulty.

The girl could only swallow and nod.

"Is your hubby a battle-fatiguer—I mean, does he wear his uniform instead of a bathrobe like the surgeries?"

"I know he wears his Army uniform because just the other day he wrote me—"

"Okay, okay. Why don't you enter your kid in our USO training course for babies? We teach 'em so they're never a disappointment to their dads. The kids just love it too. You leave her with me for awhile and quit your worrying. What's her name?"

"Mabel."

"Come along, Mabel," said Marge unemotionally. "Want to see the wheels of a watch go round and round?"

Mabel, a four-year-old with pale yellow hair and dark blue eyes, stared at the steady bulk of Marge for a full minute, then climbed down from her mother's lap, and took hold of the warm, rough hand held out to her.

"Hey you, Sammy," Marge called across to a tall sailor with his arm in a sling, "See that the missus here," jerking her head toward Mabel's mother, "gets a cup of coffee and some of that mocha cake, will you? Bet she'd like to sit at that bright sunny table way in the back." Marge glanced at the child, gave Sammy an elaborate wink, and managed to convey to him the idea that mother and child were to be separated for a little while. Good-naturedly Sammy took the cue.

"Now which of you boys has got a watch with a back that opens?" inquired Marge leading her charge into the midst of a group of Army uniforms.

From that point on the thing took care of itself with the men vying with each other to entertain the child. After two or three mornings of this Mabel took for granted that anyone in uniform was her friend. Then the day for visiting her father came and Marge whooped with joy when she was told afterwards that Mabel had run straight into his arms and that he had cried, "She knew me! My kid knew me right off the bat!"

Meanwhile the USO was branching out in its program for convalescents. A special committee on home hospitality had been set up in line with a new development in many parts of the country. People near these hospital areas were generous about offering their grounds, their swimming pools and private beaches, picture galleries, saddle horses, tennis courts, and golf courses—any private recreation facilities they might have in secluded areas where the men would be free from general public scrutiny.

Patients showing no outward disability needed special attention too. The battle-fatigue men were of this number. Picnics were a favorite form of relaxation for them, none the less so when now and then two or three would saunter off individually from the crowd. Flinging themselves down on the grass, they might fold their arms under their heads, tilt their caps over their eyes, or doze peacefully within earshot of reassuring, non-military noises: the whir of a lawnmower, the snip of hedges being trimmed, the laughing rise and fall of women's voices.

Now and then the hospital authorities would ask Mrs. Winter if Mr. and Mrs. Todd were free to take a man in for several days. These older people were a small grocer and his wife, friends of Mrs. Winter's father. They often had a lively, lovable granddaughter staying with them and in at least one instance the child herself had helped. The guest that time had been scarcely more than a youngster himself but combat had left him with a nervous speech disorder. The child, opening the door for him upon his arrival, had at once adopted him as hers. From then on they were inseparable. By the end of his stay, his speech had noticeably improved and the doctors were delighted with the change in him.

But Mr. and Mrs. Todd, even without the child's assistance, were naturals for such hospitality. They were always needing their guest's help. "Catch a-hold there, will you, Bob? We gotta get this plank up on the sawhorse if we're going to get her sawed in two, right length to reinforce the woodshed door." Or, "Could you give this egg beater a few whirls for me, Bob? Looks like my arm's about wore out and this icing's no good unless it's beaten every minute while it's cooking." Not much chance for a man to brood when he was kept so busy being a regular member of the family.

Not many weeks went by before preparations were under way for a party at the hospital. The Red Cross had asked the USO to furnish twenty-five Junior Hostesses and to provide any entertainment they wished. A small orchestra would be on hand but if the USO wanted to bring some home-made food it would be most welcome.

Careful checking ahead of time revealed that their guests that night would be in various stages of convalescence so the girls must be prepared for quiet games and talk as well as for more active participation.

"We'll need two or three older men, too," Mrs. Winter told John Richmond. "Some of these men back from combat aren't interested in

girls and dancing. They want to talk to older men about the possibilities in various kinds of business. I told Tom he'd have to go."

The party at the hospital was a formal. The Junior Hostesses, led
by one Molly McMasters, decided the men deserved the best their
wardrobes afforded. "It's their coming-out party, you know, Mrs.
Winter—the first time they've done anything with girls for a good
long time. We ought to look like people worth doing something *with*."

Molly had her way, as usual, partly because she was herself and
partly, where other girls were concerned, because she was engaged to
a young man in the Air Force who had recently been made a Colonel.
The prestige she was to have among the hospital men was due to the
first fact plus a report that her brother, a plain GI, had been killed on
Bataan and posthumously decorated.

The formal did not get off to the flying start Molly had intended.
The boys at first were embarrassed because the girls were so dressed
up while they had on their regulation, dark red robes. Even those so
anxious to dance their feet kept time with the orchestra, stood in a
line along the wall.

Mrs. Winter, in dark red herself with touches of gold kid, saw at
once what the trouble was. She gave an order to Molly to be relayed
to the other girls and on the rare occasions when Mrs. Winter ordered,
she was obeyed. She then asked the orchestra leader if he would stop
a minute and give her a chance to make a speech. He did so with a
series of lively chords that riveted everyone's attention.

"This is the USO's first party at the hospital," she said as naturally
as though she had intended all along making a few introductory remarks. "A few of you we've already had a chance to welcome at the
club. When you come to see us there, as we hope all of you will soon
and often, you will find us in our everyday working clothes. But here
tonight, welcoming most of you back to this country for the first time,
we wanted to show in some special way our appreciation of all you've
done. We know that you yourselves couldn't be wearing more honor-

able clothes than you have on tonight. To match you as nearly as we can, we've put on our very nicest dresses. We hope you like them but most of all we hope you have a lot of fun!"

Her way of saying it, both sincere and gay, brought spontaneous applause. The orchestra swung into their liveliest music and the girls, dancing with each other, swept out upon the floor. This sight, together with Mrs. Winter's reassuring words, was too much for masculine sidelines. The men made a dash for partners and the active section of the evening was suddenly in full swing.

Meanwhile patients in wheelchairs had rolled themselves in to see the fun and to their surprise found they had Junior Hostess partners for the evening just as the dancers had. One of them, a rather sullen-looking man with wavy red hair and a blanket dragging a little on the floor in front but tucked firmly behind his back at the waist, drew the best-looking girl at the party. His surprise startled a protest out of him. "Look here, don't bother about me. Get along there and hoof it with the whole boys."

"You may be surprised, mister," she told him sweetly, offering him a cigarette and then lighting it for him with a smart little flourish, "but I don't care about being turned down so flat. There's a contest on in about two minutes and I need a partner—a smart partner—if we're to win it as I mean us to. Meanwhile," she opened her bag, "I'm a handwriting expert. How about having a look at yours?"

He did not reply but she paid no attention to his silence and handed him a used envelope from her bag and a pencil. In childish round letters, obviously not his natural hand, he wrote *John Q. Doe*.

"My turn now." Taking the pencil she wrote *Jane Q. Doe* underneath in exact imitation of his. "Now it's my turn again," she went on, "and I'm going to guess how you would write your name really if your name really were that!"

While he watched, interested in spite of himself, she executed three different and impressive signatures.

"You're a nut," he stated looking, however, somewhat less solemn.

"Here, give me that" and taking the pencil he dashed off something not too legible but definite and strong which he said was Henry Nottingham.

"Good evening, Mr. Nottingham."

"Good evening, Miss Patricia Newton," and at her look of surprise, he laughed.

"You saw it on the other side of the envelope," she guessed.

Then the contest was under way. From a Junior Hostess dressed as a page, she received a large paper shopping bag similar to those being given each Junior Hostess. To her partner she explained that when the word GO was given, he was to begin making her a hat out of its contents.

"Me? Make a woman's hat? You make it!"

Patricia shook her head, ignoring his distress but observing he was noticing similar reactions in his nearby fellow patients. "All I get to do is be the model." As she spoke she began emptying the bag: one large artificial rose—glaringly red—a dish mop, a small pie plate, a roll of wire, some pliers and wire-cutters, a small roll of adhesive tape, and a length of frilled shelf paper.

"Out of *that?*" he fairly shrieked.

"Yeah," thoughtfully. "We didn't draw such a hot collection of material, did we? This is going to take a couple of good stout brain waves."

Suddenly it struck him funny. Suddenly he was terribly keen to do something about this nonsense. "Look," he said, "do we have to use every single piece of this stuff?"

"Oh no. All we have to do is make the best-looking hat at the party."

"Hand me those pliers. Am I going to make you a honey!"

And he did. There was something about the pert upsweep of the carefully bent tin pan, about the angle of the outrageous rose, and the flutter of white paper lace behind, that put his achievement, when mounted on her head, far out in front of all the rest when the models paraded carefully before the GI judges.

"Goodie!" cried Patricia with unaffected pleasure when they were awarded first place. And Henry's grin hadn't a trace of bitterness. The prize was a large home-made cake with caramel icing in generous swaths and with it on a card went one not-to-be-broken condition: "This is for the winner to take away with him. Not to be all eaten up by the party!"

"Hello, Henry! Good old Henry!" came the calls from all sides when this was read. "Be seeing you, Henry—later!"

Then the dance was on again and Patricia and Henry found they both liked chess and promptly monopolized the best-looking set in the game cupboard.

John Richmond was late in arriving. "How are things going?" he asked one of the Red Cross women as he approached the recreation hall.

"Fine on the whole. Those Junior Hostesses of yours are good. It's remarkable how sensible they are and how really friendly. But I think your contemporary, Tom Winter, is having rather hard going on the porch. Sounds to me as though the older men out there have formed a Gripe Club. Better go and lend him a hand."

It was as she had surmised. They were nearly all older married men with families and their convalescence seemed provokingly slow to them. They were full of complaints—petty and more serious. John Richmond led them on to talk, not saying much himself but managing to convey the impression that there was a good deal in what they said. He had brought along some especially good cigars and an enormous bag of peanuts in the shell, still warm from the roaster.

When he had a chance he asked if any of them would care to go through some of the factories in the vicinity. He thought he might be able to arrange it. Or would they like to have one or two personnel men come in some evening, not to make a speech but to have questions fired at them—anything they might be wondering about?

Each suggestion caught the interest of a few and served also to lead them off into less disgruntled talk. Then Tom Winter, relieved of sole responsibility for the discussion, told several funny yarns and the men generally seemed to like their section of the party.

It was not long before closing time when John Richmond caught an impression that something special was going on in the main room. Excusing himself, he went to see. The dancers had formed a ring around Molly McMasters and a lithe little sailor who were engaged in what appeared to be a solo jitterbugging exhibition. Anne Winter told him later they had been one of many couples dancing until the sailor had gone outside, removed his artificial leg, and come back to hop gleefully through the dance. Certainly the kid's balance was nearly perfect. The orchestra had slowed the tempo of the dance but as far as an observer could tell he was going through the lively routine with little support from Molly.

Abruptly the music stopped and he executed a final swagger, flushed but triumphant. A fellow patient handed him a crutch to lean on and he beamed impudently at Molly, obviously aware he had broken the rule that artificial limbs were to be worn on such occasions if only for the sake of the practice afforded.

John Richmond could see that Molly felt she had a job to do and, knowing Molly, he was not surprised when she went on with it though he suspected she wished the crowd would stop watching them. "All right, sonny. That was quite some stunt. Now go put your leg back on and we'll do it right."

"Not on your life! What do I want with that thing? It's just a nuisance."

"Snap into it, sailor. It's the only way you'll get used to it."

He didn't move and his jaw had a stubborn set. John Richmond learned afterward they had had similar trouble with him in the hospital routine. Here and there Junior Hostesses, sensing complications, moved away with their partners, easing the strain of so many spectators.

"No more dancing till you do," said Molly firmly.

"Dear mom, there are other gals."

"Not here. I'll pass the word around."

"It'd be a frame-up!"

"Yes."

John Richmond was startled to hear how tired she sounded all at once. But why shouldn't she be tired? Then he saw her give her head a toss. He saw her reach out for the sailor's hand and give him her sweetest smile. "Don't be a silly," she said. "You're only wasting time. I want to dance. Hurry back. They're already tuning up."

And through the whining slur of the violin, the *a-a-a* of the piano, and the thrum of the cello, John Richmond heard the sailor say, "Okay, sister, you win."

ALL THE WORLD'S THE S

The areas indicated with ● a